CONTENTS

Part Two: THE AFTERMATH

CONTRIBUTORS

Dr. Jacob Robinson: Coordinator of Research Activities and Publications on the Holocaust for Yad Vashem and YIVO, New York

Dr. Nira Feldman: Research Fellow in Contemporary Jewry, the Hebrew University of Jerusalem

Israel Gutman: Historian, Kibbutz Lehavot Habashan

Prof. Yehuda Bauer: Professor of Contemporary Jewry, the Hebrew University of Jerusalem

Dr. Leni Yahil: Historian, Jerusalem

Joseph Litvak: Researcher, Jerusalem

Prof. Guenter Lewy: Professor of Government, the University of Massachusetts, Amherst

Reverend John M. Snoek: Secretary of the World Council of Churches' Committee on the Church and the Jewish People, Geneva

Prof. Saul Friedländer: Professor of International Relations and Contemporary History, the Hebrew University of Jerusalem

Emmanuel Brand: Archivist, Jerusalem

Gabriel Bach: State Attorney of the State of Israel, Jerusalem

Dr. Yehoshafat Harkabi: Major General (Res.), Israel Defense Forces: Senior Lecturer in International Relations and Middle Eastern Studies, the Hebrew University of Jerusalem

Dr. Binyamin Eliav; Editor and former official, Ministry for Foreign Affairs, Jerusalem

Part One
THE HOLOCAUST

1 THE HISTORY OF THE HOLOCAUST

The "Holocaust" (also known as the Catastrophe, the Sho'ah שׁוֹאָה, the Ḥurban חֻרְבָּן) is undoubtedly the most tragic period of Jewish Diaspora history and indeed of modern mankind as a whole. It started in Germany on Jan. 30, 1933, with the accession of the Nazis to power, and ended on May 8, 1945, with the unconditional surrender of Nazi Germany. The 12 years of the Nazi anti-Jewish *Aktion* (1933–44) constitute an uninterrupted progression toward an ever-increasing radicalization of objectives and barbarization of methods in constantly expanded territories under direct Nazi control or under decisive Nazi influence, to the accompaniment of vicious, sometimes obscene, anti-Jewish propaganda. The consequences of the Holocaust are of decisive significance for the Jewish present and future: those consequences are still evident now and will be experienced for generations to come.

The nature of the Holocaust is unique. Millions of Jews—some for periods of 12 years—lived under the all-pervading Nazi power, enduring its threats and its *Aktionen*. The Jews lived in agony. Tortured by anxiety, insecure in the present, unable to anticipate the future, torn between hope and despair, they were helpless in the face of a tremendous machine always ready to crush them. The psychological effects on those who had to live through this period of total persecution are beyond even superficial description. This survey is an attempt to trace at least the external events, the extraordinary human suffering of a specially selected "race," pursued over the length and breadth of a continent and beyond, condemned to mass murder. Integrated or segregated, educated or ignorant,

Nazi Party mass rally in Nuremberg, 1933. Courtesy Schaefer Verlag, Munich.

rich or poor, young or old, every Jew was condemned. East European Jewry, however, was especially singled out, in the belief that by destroying this reservoir of Jewish population and culture, the Nazis would have the ultimate "solution" to the "Jewish question."

Two major periods of the Holocaust can be discerned: the prewar period and the period of World War II.

First Period: From the Nazi Accession to Power to the Beginning of Germany's Military Expansion (1933–39). THE NAZI ACCESSION TO POWER. On Jan. 30, 1933, the aging president of the German Republic, Paul von Hindenburg, appointed Adolf Hitler, leader of the National Socialist (Nazi) German Workers Party (NSDAP), chancellor of the Reich. The program of the party (1920), which was supposed to be "unchangeable" *("unabaenderlich"),* proclaimed the racial principle as the criterion for citizenship, and initiated the institutionalization of racial anti-Semitism

"Sieg Heil!" Mass rally in Berlin, March 1938. Courtesy Schaefer Verlag, Munich.

as a concrete governmental program. The essential characteristics of this form of anti-Semitism were: its primary importance among the objectives of the "thousand-year Reich"; its world dimensions; its implacable determinism; and its unsurpassed "consistency" and cruelty. Hitler's *Mein Kampf* (1925), the gospel of the movement and of the Nazi state, overflows with hatred and contempt for the Jews. The Nazi Party's attitude toward the Jews is expressed in the coarse slogan: *Deutschland erwache, Juda verrecke* ("Germany wake up, Judah drop dead") and in the words of the S.A. *Sturmlied: "Wenn das Judenblut vom Messer spritzt, dann geht's nochmal so gut"* ("And when Jew blood spurts from the knife, things will go twice as well"). What could be expected from the party and its affiliated organizations was demonstrated by numerous acts of violence before the seizure of power (at the hands of the Storm Troopers from 1924 on), as well as by unrestrained propaganda (books, pamphlets, and periodicals, such as *Der Stuermer,* published from 1923 on), in which the Jew was presented as a subhuman *(Untermensch),* a parasite, a phenomenon of decay *(Faeulniserscheinung),* and the main cause of all German misfortunes. "It is our duty," Hitler said in 1920, "to arouse, to whip up, and to incite in our people the instinctive repugnance of the Jews."

THE GEOGRAPHY OF THE FIRST PERIOD. The geographic expansion of Nazi anti-Jewish ideology, propaganda, and actions started with the Free City of Danzig, which was under the supervision of the League of Nations. Step by step, from 1933 on, Danzig followed Germany's lead in her racial policies, although German troops did not march into the city until Sept. 1, 1939. The Saar region was returned to Germany on March 1, 1935. In German Upper Silesia, where the Jews were under the protection of the German-Polish Convention of May 15, 1922, the restrictions imposed by the Convention on the exercise of German sovereignty terminated on July 15, 1937. This was followed by the annexation of Austria on March 13, 1938 (the so-called *Anschluss*), the annexation of the Sudetenland on Oct. 1, 1938, by virtue of the Munich Agreement, and the annexation of the Memel region on March 22, 1939 (the latter two National-Socialist, to varying degrees, long before). Also included in this period of "peaceful" expansion was the partition of the remaining part of Czechoslovakia (March 15, 1939), and the emergence of two German "protectorates" with dire consequences for the fate of the Jews: one, Bohemia-Moravia, imposed by threats, the other, Slovakia, an avowedly National Socialist state (headed by Catholic priests), "independent" by "grace of the Fuehrer." A strip of southern Slovakia and Ruthenia was ceded under German pressure by Czechoslovakia to Hungary (formally under a German-Italian arbitration award of Nov. 2, 1938), and the remainder of Ruthenia, renamed Carpatho-Ukraine, was occupied by the Hungarian army on March 15, 1939. At that time, Hungarian Jewry was already subjected to various restrictions under the anti-Jewish laws of 1938 and 1939. The Jews in all these areas were assimilated either immediately or gradually to the status of Jews in Germany and Hungary, respectively. However, the Jews of the Saar region, Upper Silesia, the Sudeten region, and Danzig had a better chance of preparing for emigration than did the Jews of Germany, Austria, and the protectorate of Bohemia-Moravia. As for Memel, the majority of its Jews found refuge in Lithuania proper and shared the fate of their brethren there.

NAZI POLICY. The aim of the Nazi policy vis-à-vis the Jews during this period was to make Germany and German-controlled areas free of Jews (judenrein). By making life unbearable, the Germans forced the Jews to emigrate. Nazi policy was to use "legal" means to "eliminate" (ausgliedern) Jews from the German state and society, assigning the racial principle as the dominant guide for the Third Reich. The Jews were eliminated from citizenship, public office, the professions, and the intellectual and artistic life of the country. Public schools were finally closed to Jewish children on Nov. 15, 1938. The regime intervened in family life (racial principle in marriages) and in personal life (*Rassenschande,* or "desecration of the race") under the Nuremberg Law of Sept. 15, 1935, "for the protection of German blood and German honor." Under this law 2,000 people were sentenced during 1936–39. The Citizenship Law of the same date stipulated that Jews could not be citizens of the Reich *(Reichsbuerger).* A series of economic measures were adopted: various restrictions on, and "aryanization" of, major Jewish concerns; locally enforced sales of property and business;

The Berlin boycott of Jewish shops, June 1933. Courtesy Yad Vashem Archives, Jerusalem. Photo Landesbiltstelle, Berlin.

The burning of books, May 10, 1933. The sign on the truck says, "German students march against the un-German spirit." Photo Ullstein, Berlin.

nationwide registration of Jewish property (April 26, 1938); registration and marking of Jewish-owned businesses—*juedisches Geschaeft* (June 14, 1938); aryanization and/or liquidation of Jewish-owned retail businesses (Nov. 12, 1938) and of industrial enterprises (Dec. 3, 1938); and full-scale spoliation of Jewish property and businesses leading to pauperization of the Jewish population. In addition, the regime enforced personal isolation and ostracism. The first census on a racial basis was on May 17, 1938; Jews were forced to adopt the added names Sara or Israel on Aug. 17, 1938; the letter "J" was stamped on passports in accordance with the decree of Oct. 5, 1938, following a suggestion by Swiss authorities; compulsory identification cards were issued from Jan. 1, 1939.

Nor was there a lack of acts of degradation and violence throughout Germany: the April 1, 1933, institution of the boycott; the burning of Jewish and various non-Jewish authors' books on May 10, 1933; spiriting off

Kristallnacht in Baden-Baden. On Nov. 10, 1938, Jewish men are rounded up by the police and marched through the city. Courtesy Yad Vashem Archives, Jerusalem.

Kristallnacht, November 9–10, 1938. The burning of the synagogue of Landau in der Pfalz. Courtesy Landau Municipality.

of numerous Jews to concentration camps (e.g., those sentenced for *Rassenschande* by the secret order of June 12, 1937, and returning emigrants by the Gestapo order of Jan. 23, 1938); atrocities committed against Jews following the *Anschluss;* the June 15, 1938, *Aktion,* in which 1,500 Jews were taken to concentration camps; the *Kristallnacht* ("night of broken glass") of Nov. 9–10, 1938, preceded by the deportation of some 15,000 to 17,000

Polish Jews in the direction of the Polish border station Zbaszyn (Oct. 28, 1938), and by "dress rehearsals" in Bavaria (destruction of the Munich synagogue on June 9, 1938, and of the Nuremberg synagogue on Aug. 10, 1938). There was also violence of a local nature, as, e.g., the anti-Jewish riots by the S.A. in Berlin (March 9 and 10, 1933); destruction of two Jewish-owned department stores in Braunschweig on March 11, 1933; chasing of Jewish judges and lawyers from the Breslau court on March 13, 1933; "Jews not wanted" *(Juden unerwuenscht)* signs on businesses, cafés, sport stadiums, and roads leading into towns and resorts; scratching out *(herauskratzen)* the names of Jewish war dead from memorials in some places; savage anti-Jewish propaganda of hatred and contempt, including the *"Stuermer"* boxes all over the country.

In the short period of some six and a half years, the 2,000-year-old German-Jewish community, numbering half

Inside the Baden-Baden synagogue the men, having been made to remove their hats, have to listen to one of the congregation, Mr. Dreyfus, reading the *Stuermer* from the pulpit and to repeat the response, "It is true, we are a dirty, filthy people." The S.S. also forced them to sing Nazi songs and do gymnastic exercises. Courtesy Yad Vashem Archives, Jerusalem.

a million in 1933 (including foreign and stateless Jews), was uprooted and reduced to a group of some 220,000 outlaws who could expect nothing but continued persecution and harassment, and finally deportation to death.

THE EXPANSION OF GERMAN INFLUENCE TO OTHER COUNTRIES. The establishment of the Nazi regime came at a time when the nations of East and Central Europe were involved in a crisis of democratic institutions, and the emergence of nationalist and authoritarian parties was aided by Nazi support. The anti-Jewish policies of Germany openly flouted generally accepted canons of behavior toward minorities. Failure by the world to react served as a signal to other states, which, although treaty-bound to protect minorities, followed the German example. The result was a significant interplay of indigenous anti-Semitism and willingly imported Nazi theories and practices. Anti-Jewish discriminatory measures were adopted and anti-Jewish propaganda increased considerably during this

Hitler Youth forcing Vienna Jews to scrub the streets, November 1938. Courtesy B. M. Ansbacher, Jerusalem.

The "New Order." Courtesy Yad Vashem Archives, Jerusalem.

period. Organized anti-Semitism everywhere received strong encouragement from Nazi Germany.

Hungary followed the example set by German discriminatory legislation, which was extended to the territories lost under the Trianon Treaty and recovered with Germany's help (part of southern Slovakia and Carpatho-Ukraine). Acts of violence against Jews, who were considered to be loyal to Czechoslovakia, occurred in the course of the Hungarian occupation. In Rumania, Hitler's accession to power, his impressive diplomatic triumphs, and the affinity of strong anti-Jewish groups to National Socialism, spurred and encouraged indigenous anti-Semitism. German anti-Jewish propaganda also registered successes in Poland, Lithuania, and Latvia, through increase of governmental and economic anti-Semitism; in France, through increased anti-Jewish propaganda; and in Italy, which relinquished its opposition to anti-Semitism in 1938, adopting Germany's racial principles.

12

ATTITUDES OF GERMANS. The attitude of the German people toward the Nazi policy vis-à-vis their Jewish fellow-citizens ranged from wholehearted support and enthusiasm by the majority on ideological and economic grounds, through apathy, to individual acts of humanity. In this respect, the Germany of the 1930s was different from that of the 1880s, when anti-Semitism had been revived, particularly in Berlin. Then, a group of 75 distinguished citizens had protested solemnly against the new wave of anti-Semitism. No such protest was forthcoming in 1932 and 1933 when such protests were not impossible. Nor did the Churches raise their voices. The majority of the Protestant churches accepted the racial principles, although the dissident Confessing Church (Bekenntniskirche) took a strong stand against racism (March 17, 1935, followed by the arrest of some 700 ministers) and persisted in it. Outstanding among the registered cases of Catholic protests in this period is that of Dompropst (canon) Bernhard Lichtenberg, who, after the Kristallnacht (which incidentally elicited no protest from any German church), used to pray daily in the Hedwigskirche, Berlin, for all the persecuted.

ATTITUDE OF GERMAN JEWRY. Germany's highly assimilated Jewry (in some Jewish circles the German-Jewish relationship was defined as deutsch-juedische Symbiose) was shocked and bewildered by the incessant "legal" measures, acts of violence, and shrill voices of anti-Jewish propaganda. The demographic picture showed signs of drastically accelerated decline, mortality far exceeding births. For years German Jews grasped for the hope of a possibility of continued Jewish existence in Nazi Germany, which turned out to be illusory. They undertook measures of self-help that included vocational training and retraining, establishment of the Juedischer Kulturbund, and centralization of Jewish representation in the Reichsvertretung. The latter frequently exhorted the Jews to resoluteness and self-confidence.

Along with this trend, there existed what turned out to be 13 a much more realistic opinion which recognized that there was no hope for Jews in Germany, that expulsion was only a matter of time, and that consequently the solution was emigration. Palestine was the goal for a part of this group, helped by the Ha'avara agreement of 1933. During this period, some 280,000 Jews emigrated, despite the psychological difficulties inherent in such a decision for a community deeply rooted in Germany, and notwithstanding the limitations on emigration (e.g., the immigration quota law in the U.S., the White Paper of 1939 on Palestine, and restrictive action by most European governments). While the official Nazi German line was to get rid of the Jews, the potential emigrant had to overcome various difficulties. More "efficient" emigration procedures (including threats of internment in concentration camps, followed by actual internment) were instituted only in 1938.

Vested with practically unlimited powers, Adolf Eichmann had become, at this stage, the "grand dispatcher" of the Jews of "Greater Germany." He worked through the Zentralstelle fuer juedische Auswanderung, established in Vienna on Aug. 20, 1938, which was followed by the Reichszentrale fuer juedische Auswanderung in Berlin (Jan. 24, 1939), and the Zentralstelle fuer juedische Auswanderung in Prague (July 26, 1939). These government offices were established in order to accelerate emigration and to appropriate Jewish assets. Moreover, the Nazis believed that emigration worked to Germany's political advantage by expanding the bounds of aggressive anti-Semitism. The arrival of poor Jewish immigrants was expected to provoke anti-Jewish reactions in the countries of immigration and thus serve German interests.

WORLD JEWRY AND THE EVENTS IN CENTRAL EUROPE. Jewish communities everywhere outside Germany followed the events in Nazi Germany and its satellites with ever-increasing anxiety. Their activities were concentrated on urging their national governments to admit Jewish refugees from Germany, caring for such refugees as arrived, counteracting worldwide Nazi anti-Jewish propaganda, and carrying on world publicity on events in the ever-expanding Third Reich. On the international level, Jewish organizations pressed unsuccessfully for the adoption by the Assembly of the League of Nations (1933) of a resolution confirming the principle of protection of minorities and obliquely condemning Germany for her treatment of the Jews. They initiated the Bernheim Petition in the League of Nations, whose successful conclusion suspended the application of German racial laws in Upper Silesia for over four years. They pressed for action by the Assembly of the League of Nations in favor of "refugees from Germany, Jewish and others," and for the appointment of a High Commissioner to protect the refugees and investigate possibilities for their emigration. This last effort, along with the special conference in Evian (July 6-16, 1938), proved useless. A boycott of German goods and services was spontaneously begun by Jews in various countries, but it lacked a worldwide apparatus and its influence on the German economy was of no decisive consequence.

Second Period: From the Invasion of Poland to the Defeat of Germany. With Hitler's invasion of Poland on Sept. 1, 1939, the second period of Nazi anti-Jewish policy and practice started. It was characterized by accelerated lawlessness, pauperization, harassment, and ultimately mass murder of the Jewish population in "Greater Germany" as well as in Nazi-occupied and -influenced areas. The purpose at first was to inflict a slow death on the Jewish community. The entire program was accompanied by vicious propaganda and acts of violence at the cost of thousands of human lives. It culminated during the 1941-44 period in mass extermination of millions by shooting and gassing followed in 1945 by starvation, forced labor, and death marches of the miserable remnants, under the code name "Final Solution."

THE ELEMENTS SPECIFIC TO THE JEWISH SITUATION. The Jewish situation during the war, if compared with the Nazi treatment of Poles, Russians, non-Soviet Communists, and gypsies, was unique in these elements: (1) The destructive will *(Vernichtungswille)* of the Nazis was aimed at the 15

S.S. men amuse themselves by kicking a Jew. Poland, c. 1939–40.
Courtesy Yad Vashem Archives, Jerusalem.

totality of the Jews as Jews, and consequently the victims
included women, children, and old people, while it was
directed at only a part of the other groups. (2) The "Final
Solution" for the Jews was to be achieved immediately,
during the war, whereas decisions on the ultimate fate of
other peoples were postponed till after victory. (3) Hitler's
war against the Jews had priority over his war against all
other enemies. (4) In the Jewish case alone there was an
absence of inhibitions or conflicting considerations, which
played a role in Nazi persecution of non-Jews. Thus, despite
the critical manpower situation, particularly in the armament industry, the directive was given (although not
entirely obeyed) in December 1941 by the Ministry for the
Occupied Eastern Territories that "as a matter of principle
(grundsaetzlich) no consideration should be given to
economic interests *(Belange)*." In another critical area, the
shortage of rolling stock, Himmler and Eichmann indefa-

Poland, c. 1939–40. Courtesy Yad Vashem Archives, Jerusalem.

tigably insisted that despite urgent requirements by the
armed forces, priority should be given to deportations.
Indeed, here the insatiable destructive will of the Nazis
reached apocalyptic dimensions.

THE GEOGRAPHY OF THE SECOND PERIOD. The area in
which anti-Jewish measures were imposed is commensurate
with the ever-expanding territorial and political German
power: following Sept. 1, 1939, they applied to Poland;
April 9, 1940, Denmark and Norway; May 10, 1940, the
Netherlands, Belgium, Luxembourg, and France (reaching
out to French North Africa and the French Levant); Sept.
8, 1943, the day of partial occupation by German troops,
Italy (the anti-Jewish action in Libya started much earlier,
on May 2, 1942); April 6, 1941, Yugoslavia and Greece;
June 22, 1941, the U.S.S.R. in its expanded boundaries. The
war between the U.S. and Japan affected the Jews who had
found refuge in Japanese-dominated areas of Asia, especially those in Shanghai.   **17**

Areas of Nazi Persecution and Extermination in Europe, 1939–45

1. "Greater Germany," on Sept. 1, 1939, embraced Germany,
   Sudetenland, Austria, and the Protectorate of Bohemia and
   Moravia
2. General Government, occupied Poland not incorporated into
   Germany
3. Eastern Galicia, attached to U.S.S.R. in Sept. 1939, occupied
   by Germany in June 1941, and attached to the General Government in Aug. 1941
4. Western Polish areas incorporated into Germany
5. Lithuania (including Vilna region), incorporated into U.S.S.R.
   in Aug. 1940, occupied by Germany June 1941
6. Latvia, see Lithuania
7. Estonia, see Lithuania
8. Parts of Polish Belorussia, first incorporated into the U.S.S.R.
   in Sept. 1939, occupied by Germany in June 1941

9. Bialystok and Ciechanow regions under the authority of Erich Koch as *Gauleiter* of East Prussia

10. *Reichskommissariat* Ukraine, embraced former Polish Volhynia, the Pinsk region, parts of Soviet Ukraine, and Crimea

11. The U.S.S.R. areas under German military administration

12. Rumania minus ceded territories: Bessarabia, northern Bukovina and Transylvania

13. Bessarabia and northern Bukovina, ceded by Rumania to U.S.S.R. in June 1940, occupied by Rumanian and German troops in June 1941

14. Transnistria, under Rumanian administration

15. Slovakia minus area ceded to Hungary

16. Hungary enlarged by annexations

17. Bulgaria proper and southern Dobruja, ceded by Rumania

18. Bulgarian-occupied southern Serbia (Macedonia), Skoplje, Bitolj, Greek Macedonia, and Greek western Thrace

19. Northern Greece with Salonica, under German occupation

20. Southern Greece and the Greek islands, under Italian occupation from April 1941 and German occupation from Sept. 1943

21. Serbia proper and Banat, under German military and/or civilian administration

22. Northern Slovenia, under German civilian administration from April 1941, incorporated into Germany on Oct. 1, 1942

23. "Independent" Croatia, including Bosnia and Herzegovina

24. Southern Slovenia, occupied and partly annexed by Italy

25. Dalmatia, part of Dalmatian Islands, and Montenegro, occupied by Italy

26. Italy

27. Belgium, under German occupation

28. The Netherlands, under German occupation

29. Luxembourg, occupied, later annexed, by Germany

30. Alsace-Lorraine, de facto annexed by Germany

31. France, occupied by Germany in June 1941

32. Vichy France, occupied by Germany in Nov. 1942

33. Southeastern France, occupied by Italy in Nov. 1942–Sept. 1943

34. Denmark, under German occupation

35. Norway, under German occupation

Along with these military successes, Germany's political influence in Europe expanded and was strengthened by the accession to the Three-Power Agreement of Hungary (Nov. 20, 1940), Rumania (Nov. 23, 1940), Slovakia (Nov. 24, 1940), Bulgaria (March 1, 1941), and Croatia (June 15, 1941). Thirty-eight geographical areas of persecution and extermination were created with the expansion of German sovereignty to parts of Poland, France, and Yugoslavia; the occupation by Germany and her satellites of most areas of Europe and some sections of Africa and Asia; and the partition of states (see map).

A distinction is to be made, insofar as the Jewish situation is concerned, between areas annexed or occupied by Germany and those annexed or occupied by Italy. The rapid destructive process in areas under German control, e.g., in German-occupied Greece and German-occupied areas of Yugoslavia, contrasts strongly with Italian (and Albanian) humanity in Italian- and Albanian-controlled areas of Yugoslavia and the Italian-occupied French border zone. Under constant German pressure, the Italians, in the wake of Ribbentrop's[1] personal intervention with Mussolini,[2] agreed to establish concentration camps for Jews in its military zone of Croatia and on the Dalmatian Islands, but the treatment of the inmates was humane. Jewish refugees fleeing France and Yugoslavia found friendly reception from the Italian people.

All the satellites did the "preparatory work" for the Final Solution on their own, with German inspiration and guidance, and some even had special commissioners for Jewish affairs (France—Xavier Vallat, followed by Louis Darquier de Pellepoix and du Paty de Clam; Rumania—Radu Lecca; Bulgaria—Alexander Belev, followed by Khristo Stomaniakov; the Fascist Italian Republic (after 1943)—Giovanni Preziosi). However, a distinction must be made between German-created satellites (Slovakia and Croatia), and German allies with an existence of their own and possibly also with a political-military alternative. While

[1] Reich minister for foreign affairs   [2] 'Duce': or dictator of Italy

the former actively participated in the destruction of their Jews on the spot or in their deportation to the death camps, the latter were more circumspect. Moreover, consideration was apparently given to those Jews who were citizens and were culturally integrated with the majority.

Thus, in non-occupied France the government at first refused to deliver Jews of French citizenship (but not stateless Jews) for deportation. In Bulgaria, the Jews of Bulgaria proper remained practically intact, although Sofia Jews and Jews from three other towns were displaced and removed to the provinces, and Jewish property was confiscated. However, in the Bulgarian-occupied Greek and Yugoslav territories, the Jews were shipped to the East, mostly to Treblinka. In Rumania, a country where the most cruel pogroms took place in Dorohoi, Jassy, Bucharest, and Odessa following occupation by Rumanian-German troops, the Jews of the Regat and southern Transylvania remained substantially unharmed, these areas being far away from the war front and consequently from German influence. As for the Jews from the other provinces with German military presence, they were shipped not to the Polish extermination camps but to Transnistria, ostensibly for forced labor, and 40 per cent of them survived, a higher percentage than that in the Polish-Soviet area. Hungary, notorious for its Jewish labor battalions, deported some 12,000 allegedly non-Hungarian Jews to the German-administered Ukraine as early as August 1941 in full knowledge of the fate awaiting them, and Hungarian local occupation authorities shot some 4,000 Serbian Jews (along with 6,000 Serbs) in Novi Sad, without authorization from Budapest. However, Hungary did not give in to German demands for total deportation of Hungarian Jewish citizens prior to the entry of the German army on March 19, 1944 (and with it that of the Eichmann *Kommando*), and the Jews in Budapest remained largely unharmed. In Italy, even the Fascist republican government had practically no part in the deportations to Auschwitz, which were a purely German project. The Jews in Finland, a military but not a political ally of Nazi Germany, remained largely unaffected by the alliance.

A further distinction may be made between areas where the process of physical destruction was sudden, begun with the Nazi invasion (e.g., the U.S.S.R., Serbia), and such areas as the General Government and Polish areas annexed by Germany, where the systematic process of physical destruction followed the September 1939–April 1942 period. In the latter areas during this initial period, Jews were deprived of elementary human rights, including freedom of movement; robbed of their properties and businesses; dismissed from the professions, crowded in ghettos under outrageously primitive conditions; and subjected to humiliation (the yellow badge), to forced labor without remuneration, and to starvation and savage brutality. Jewish secular and religious representatives and institutions were singled out as particular targets, e.g., burning of synagogues, desecration of Torah scrolls and other ritual objects, ridiculing of rabbis. As a result, the Jews of this area entered the period of the "Final Solution" physically exhausted, morally undermined, isolated from the world (both near and far), and abandoned to the destructive will of the Nazis and their accomplices.

THE IDEA OF THE PHYSICAL DESTRUCTION OF THE JEWS AND THE EVOLUTION OF THE NAZI EXTERMINATION POLICY. The role of German scholarship in the development of the idea of physical destruction of Jews as a method of a "solution of the Jewish question" should not be underestimated. Some highlights were Eugen Duehring's suggestion of such a solution in his popular volume *Die Judenfrage* (1881); the rejection of the idea of humanitarianism by German scholars and authors (e.g., Paul de Lagarde in his *Programm fuer die konservative Partei Preussens* (1884), reproduced in his *Deutsche Schriften* (1937), 423: "We have to break with the idea of humanity"); characterization of humanity as sheer silliness *(Humanitaetsduselei)*, and the perversion, extension, and active application to human society of the Darwinian principle of natural selection in justification of the killing off *(ausmerzen)* of human beings deemed "inferior" by the "theorists."

Nazi anti-Semitism was considering this idea from its inception. As early as 1919, Hitler declared somewhat vaguely that the ultimate objective of his anti-Semitism was "the removal of the Jews altogether." In his *Mein Kampf* he expressed the view that World War I might not have been lost by Germany had "some twelve or fifteen thousand of the Hebrew corruptors of the people *(hebraeische Volksverderber)* been poisoned by gas before or during the war." The number of public declarations to this effect, not necessarily connected with the planned war, increased after the November *Kristallnacht*. At a high-level meeting chaired by Hermann Goering[3] on Nov. 12, 1938, he said: "Should the Reich become involved in an international conflict in the foreseeable future, we in Germany will obviously have to think about settling our accounts with the Jews." Two weeks later (Nov. 24, 1938), he was echoed by *Das Schwarze Korps,* the official S.S. organ: "If things were to develop in this way we would be faced with the harsh necessity of having to exterminate the Jewish underworld in just the same manner as we are used to exterminating criminals in our Order State: with fire and sword. The result would be the actual and definite end of Jewry in Germany—its complete destruction." On Jan. 21, 1939, Hitler declared to the Czech ambassador, František Chvalkovsky: "The Jews will be destroyed here," and on Jan. 30, 1939, he declared: "Today I want to be a prophet once more: If international-finance Jewry inside and outside of Europe should succeed once more in plunging nations into another world war, the consequences . . . the annihilation of the Jewish race in Europe." This statement, which was widely ignored, disbelieved, or considered a mere figure of speech, was repeated by Hitler again and again.

NAZI IDEAS FOR A TERRITORIAL "SOLUTION OF THE JEWISH QUESTION." The Nazis did have ideas about territorial concentration of Jews in wartime (the Nisko and

---

[3] Nazi field-marshal and leader

Lublin "reservations") and after the anticipated peace with France (the Madagascar Plan). The essentials of the latter plan was deportation of 4,000,000 Jews within four years after the war to live in a police state as forced laborers, under the supervision of German masters (the R.S.H.A.). The plan was to be financed by world Jewry. The project, however, was soon shelved .

SECRECY AND DECEPTION. The fact of deliberate physical destruction of human beings, and particularly of the European Jews, was never mentioned in published Nazi documents. One exception, though, was the Himmler-Thierack (Reich minister of justice) agreement of Sept. 18, 1942, in accordance with which all Jews, as well as certain other categories of people, who had been sentenced by a court and were serving in a penal institution, were to be transferred to the custody of the *Reichsfuehrer-SS* Heinrich Himmler for exploitation as expendable manpower and, according to the document, "in order to be worked to death *(zur Vernichtung durch Arbeit)*." Unlike other secret Fuehrer orders, the Final Solution order was never put in

Mass execution. Lithuania, c. 1940. Courtesy Yad Vashem
Archives, Jerusalem.

writing and apparently was given orally by Hitler to Himmler.

The evolution of the Final Solution began with Goering's order to Reinhard Heydrich (Jan. 24, 1939) concerning the solution of the Jewish question by "emigration" and "evacuation." Heydrich's instructions to the *Einsatzgruppen* (mobile S.S. units assigned to combat the civilian enemy by various methods, including mass murder) in Poland vaguely mentioned the *Endziel*, "the final objective" (Sept. 21, 1939). The March–April 1941 agreement between the high command of the German army and the *Reichsfuehrer-SS* outlined the mission of the *Einsatzgruppen* in the areas of anticipated German-Soviet hostilities. The July 31, 1941, extension of the "total solution" *(Gesamtloesung)* to all areas under German influence was carried out under Goering's order to Heydrich. A meeting of high-ranking government and party officials was held on Jan. 20, 1942 (the Wannsee Conference) to coordinate the activities of all agencies concerned with the Final Solution and the methods to be used. (The expression

Mass execution. Photograph taken from a German prisoner of war.

used in regard to the Jews was that they be "appropriately dealt with"—*entsprechend behandelt*).

The secrecy of the "operation" was scrupulously guarded. Correspondence on the Final Solution was classified top secret *(geheime Reichssache)*. On Sept. 25, 1941, a strict order from Hitler, reformulating a similar order issued at the beginning of 1940 and in effect since then, emphasized the need for absolute secrecy. Various devices were used to insure secrecy *(Geheimnisschutz)*. The participants in the operation had to sign a special oath of absolute secrecy *(unbedingte Verschwiegenheit)*. Sophisticated methods of deception, fraud, and camouflage *(Tarnung)*, devices for presenting actions as harmless *(Verharmlosung)*, and the special rules for the use of language *(Sprachregelung)* were employed to prevent the victims and world from learning of the massacres. The secrecy was complete and, to a large extent, effective. The very monstrosity of the crime made it unbelievable. In fact, the Nazis speculated that the unimaginability of their *Aktionen* would work in their favor. Commenting on a report of such an *Aktion,* Heinrich Lohse, Nazi commissioner for Ostland, observed: "Just imagine what would happen if such occurrences became known to the enemy and were exploited; but probably such propaganda would have no effect, since those who hear or read it would not be willing to believe it!" Taking no chances, the Germans initiated "Operation Blot Out" *(Spurverwischung)* by *Kommando 1005* under *SS-Standartenfuehrer* Paul Blobel in 1942, in which mass graves were opened up and the remains burned. This operation was continued for many months everywhere in the East. Despite all the efforts, Himmler's expectation that "the extermination of the Jewish people . . . this glorious chapter of our history . . . should never be told" was frustrated by the Allied victory. Nazi archives were opened, contemporary Jewish documents were discovered, and facts were ferreted out by courts and scholars. Moreover, by 1942 the Free World had gradually learned the truth, albeit not always complete and precise.

Nomadization and Temporary Living Quarters. Among the phenomena of the period that have direct implications for the Final Solution, two are to be emphasized: the nomadization of millions of persons, and the particular forms of temporary dwellings in this period. The Jews became an uprooted people, on the move. Emigration was reduced to a trickle and was stopped altogether on Oct. 1, 1941. Instead, panicky flights from the Nazi terror in search of shelter became the rule. Inside the areas of persecution, the flight was partly voluntary (from small towns to larger cities), but largely enforced in accordance with the Nazi plans for the concentration of the Jews in a small number of ghettos. The flight from areas considered unsafe to places with some promise of safety encompassed Jews from the "Greater German" area fleeing to Yugoslavia; Polish Jews fleeing to the Soviet Union, Hungary, and Rumania; Hungarian Jews to Rumania; Slovakian Jews to Hungary, and later Hungarian Jews to Slovakia; Yugoslav Jews to Italy and Albania; Belgian, Luxembourg, and Dutch Jews to France and Switzerland, and in some cases to England; French Jews fleeing from the occupied zone to the "free" one, then to Spain or the Italian zone, then to the Swiss border. Thousands of Jews drifted on the high seas for months in ramshackle boats under wretched conditions before a friendly harbor was moved to receive them. Many became ill through starvation, neglect, and despair, and many committed suicide. Among the "death ships" were the *Struma* (1942) and the *Mefkure* (1944), which both sank in the Black Sea.

While there might have been an element of self-interest for the migrant, nothing of the sort can be said about the deportations of Austrian and Czech Jews to the Nisko "reservation" (from September 1939 to the spring of 1940); of German, Austrian, Czech, and Luxembourg Jews to Lodz, Warsaw, Kovno (Kaunas), Riga, and Minsk; of Jews from the "Greater German" Reich (including Wartheland) and from the General Government to Lublin, which, under Odilo Globocnik, became the operational center of 27 the *Aktion Reinhard* (named for Reinhard Heydrich) and the site of three extermination camps; of able-bodied Jews (called *Makkabaeer*) from one place to another; and, above all, of the mass deportation of Jews from all of Europe to the death camps. Of a different nature was the deportation by the U.S.S.R., on the eve of the German invasion, of Jews, along with other "disloyal" elements, from the newly-gained Polish, Rumanian, and Baltic territories to the east of that country. Although it was intended as a police measure against persons allegedly "hostile" to the new regime, the Soviet deportation in many cases turned out in favor of the deportees who thus became removed from an area that would soon be Nazi dominated.

The specific forms of segregated or isolated Jewish temporary quarters imposed by the Nazis, all resulting from large-scale dislocations of the Jewish population, were: (1) ghettos; (2) internment (transit) camps used after manhunts, mostly for deportation (in occupied France—Pithiviers, Beaune-la-Rolande, Compiègne, Drancy; in non-occupied France alien Jews were concentrated in Gurs and Rivesaltes; in Serbia—Topovske Šupe in Belgrade, Šabac, and Sajmište in Belgrade; in Croatia—Jasenovac; in the Netherlands— Westerbork, Vught; in Belgium— Breendonck, Dassin-Malines); (3) labor camps (see chap. 3). Jews who were trying to flee from camps and ghettos found temporary shelter in bunkers and with partisan units in the woods. A category apart were the Jews in hiding with Christian neighbors on the "Aryan side" in Poland (parts of cities in Poland reserved for the "Aryan" population, as opposed to the ghetto areas where all Jews were confined).

These quarters constituted another factor in the continuing process that also included pauperization, forced labor (in the Polish-Soviet area, Hungary, Rumania, Slovakia, Bulgaria, Croatia, and Germany from March 7, 1941), starvation ("... we have condemned 1.2 million Jews to death through hunger..." Hans Frank), illness, and epidemics. Thus in Warsaw, 43,239 Jews (out of a total of some 450,000) died during the last year before resettlement (1941). In the Theresienstadt ghetto, partly an *Alterghetto* (ghetto for old people), 33,521 Jews died out of a total of 140,937. In the "privileged" camp of Bergen-Belsen, some 14,000 Jewish inmates died shortly after the liberation, in addition to 36,000 persons, mostly sick, brought from labor and concentration camps, who died before liberation from exhaustion and epidemics. In the Polish areas, prior to deportation to death camps there were executions of individuals and large groups (sometimes the total Jewish population of a place), accounting for many tens of thousands of victims.

ORGANS OF IMPLEMENTATION OF THE FINAL SOLUTION, ESPECIALLY EINSATZGRUPPEN AND DEATH CAMPS. The chief executors of the Final Solution were the *Reichsfuehrer-SS* and chief of German police, Heinrich Himmler, and his lieutenant, Reinhard Heydrich, chief of security police *(Chef der Sicherheitspolizei und des SD)*, later followed by Ernst Kaltenbrunner (Jan. 30, 1943). Accordingly, the main implementing agency was the Security Police—its central office, the R.S.H.A. *(Reichssicherheitshauptamt)*, as well as its regional and local organizations, and in particular the department concerned with political enemies, the Gestapo (Amt IV), headed by Heinrich Mueller. Section IVB4 of this office (later IVA4b in March 1944), called Jewish Affairs, was headed by Adolf Eichmann, the *Referent* for the Final Solution, who dispatched emissaries all over occupied or controlled Europe (see chap. 9). An important role in this process was played by the S.S. and police leaders and their units in German-controlled Europe, who had jurisdiction over the extermination camps. The administration of the concentration camps, including Auschwitz and Lublin- Majdanek (Maidanek), was handled by the Main Office of the Administration of the Economy—*Wirtschaftsverwaltungshauptamt* (W.V.H.A.). The individuals involved in these *Aktionen,* and in particular the personnel of the *Einsatzgruppen* (in the U.S.S.R., these were mobile killing units), came from all branches of 29 the Security Police, from various units and agencies of the S.S., and from the *Ordnungspolizei.*

These above-mentioned were the main implementors— the agents immediately connected with the extermination process. Many other agencies and individuals, Party and governmental, cooperated to carry out the program: (1) The Chancellery of the Fuehrer of the NSDAP, which supplied the extermination camps with expertise and personnel, acquired and trained in the euthanasia operation; (2) the Foreign Office, through special department D III, headed by Martin Luther (its Jewish desk headed by Franz Rademacher), followed by Horst Wagner (Jewish desk, Eberhard von Thadden); and advisers on Jewish affairs *(Judenberater)* of the Eichmann office attached to the embassies; (3) the Reich Chancellery (Reichskanzlei); (4) the Plenipotentiary for the Four-Year Plan *(Beauftragter fuer den Vierjahresplan);* (5) the ministries of Occupied Eastern Territories, Transportation, Economics, Justice, Interior, Propaganda, and Finance; and (6) the army. In addition to these German state and party organs there were: (7) volunteer units of Russians, Ukrainians, Belorussians, Lithuanians, Latvians, Hungarians, *Volksdeutsche* (persons of German origin living outside of Germany), and others who served the Nazis both in their home countries and abroad; and (8) local government forces, such as the Ustashi (Croatian fascist units), Hlinka Guard (Slovak fascist units), the police in "Greater Germany," and police units in areas under German control, sometimes called *Hiwis-Hilfswillige,* "willing to help."

Einsatzgruppen. Einsatzgruppen der Sicherheitspolizei (und des Sicherheitsdienstes) were active immediately following the *Anschluss* of Austria, the incorporation of the Sudetenland, and the annexation by Germany of Bohemia-Moravia. Their main function was to follow the army and carry out "special tasks." In Poland their *Aktion* (Sept. 1, 1939–Oct. 25, 1939) against Poles—mainly members of the clergy, professionals, and members of the leadership group—and against Jews (known under the code name

"Bloody Wednesday" in Olkusz (Cracow district), July 31, 1940. In retaliation for the killing of a German policeman, the Nazis carried out a public mass execution of Jews. Courtesy Yad Vashem Archives, Jerusalem.

Jews executed in Lodz, Poland. Courtesy Yad Vashem Archives, Jerusalem. **31**

Operation Tannenberg) was relatively "modest" by comparison with later ones in the Soviet area, but was carried out with great violence and cruelty. Altogether there were less than 2,000 men in six *Einsatzgruppen,* including the dreaded *Einsatzgruppe* for Special Tasks (*Einsatzgruppe zur besonderen Verwendung*). The military administration too had its part in the predicament of Polish Jews (e.g., internment of civilian population, imposition of forced labor, expulsion of numerous Jews beyond the San and Narew rivers).

The *Einsatzgruppen* in the Soviet Union were larger and equipped with more authority in the field of "political and police special tasks." They were instructed orally by *SS-Brigadefuehrer* Bruno Streckenbach (on behalf of Himmler and Heydrich) to shoot all the Jews. There were altogether four of these task forces. The *Einsatzgruppen,* attached to army groups North, Center, South, and the Eleventh Army, respectively, were divided into a number of *Kommandos.* Altogether there were some 3,000 to 4,000 men, assisted by the German police, *Hiwis,* and sometimes

Building the wall of the Warsaw ghetto. Courtesy Yad Vashem Archives, Jerusalem.

Waffen-SS (front-line S.S. units from all parts of Europe) and *Feldgendarmerie* (mobile military police).

In Poland the *Einsatzgruppen* were instruments of destruction of Jewish lives prior to the establishment of civilian administration. The subordination of the *Einsatzgruppen* to the army during the Polish campaign was stronger than in the Russian campaign. There is no evidence, however, that the Wehrmacht used its power to prevent "the murder of tens of thousands of Jews and Poles," although on Feb. 6, 1940, an official document of the *Oberbefehlshaber Ost* (Supreme Commander in the East) warned that "the greatest harm . . . which will be suffered by the German people itself owing to present conditions, is the extreme brutalization and moral degeneracy which will spread among valuable German human material like pestilence in a very short time." In fact, there was even a suggestion that all police forces, together with their leaders, and all commanders attached to the organizations of the General Government, be relieved abruptly, to be replaced "with morally intact and honorable units." Nevertheless during the Russian campaign, the army's leaders, fully aware of the horrors committed by the *Einsatzgruppen,* silently acquiesced, and even approved. There were occasional exceptions in both directions: actual participation by the army in the *Einsatzgruppen Aktionen,* or encouragement of them, on the one hand, and refusal to participate in mass murder, on the other.

In the Soviet areas the shooting and occasional gassing of Jews by the *Einsatzgruppen* reached gigantic proportions during two waves of intensive extermination: the first, in the course of the hostilities (June–October 1941), and the second a few months later (from January 1942), following the stabilization of the front. The second wave was accompanied by temporary ghettoization and was carried out by the same *Kommandos,* now stationary, with the assistance of the *Hiwis.* The shootings were carried out on the spot or in the vicinity of cities and towns (e.g., Babi Yar in Kiev, Ponary in Vilna, the Ninth Fort in Kovno). While the 33

Jews in Bessarabia, Bukovina, and north Moldavia fell victim to the *Einsatzkommandos* and Rumanian army units immediately upon the invasion, a different fate was reserved for Rumanian Jews deported to Rumanian-German-occupied Transnistria, as well as for the Jews in Serbia and Croatia under German and Croatian authority: extermination, mostly in local camps. The number of unknown mass graves of the hundreds of thousands of victims, including those in the little-known extermination camps of Jungfernhof in Latvia, and Maly Trostinec near Minsk, cannot be ascertained.

The Mass Murder Centers in Poland. For the rest of European Jewry, including Poland (for the survivors of "slow death" and numerous executions in various localities) and part of the U.S.S.R., there were mass murder centers in Poland to which the victims were deported for extermination by shooting and especially by gassing. The major ones were: (1) Chelmno (Dec. 8, 1941–Jan. 18, 1945); (2) Belzec (Nov. 1, 1941–June 30, 1943); (3) Sobibor (March 1, 1942–Nov. 30, 1943); (4) Treblinka (June 1, 1942–Nov. 30, 1943); (5) Lublin-Majdanek, established Nov. 1, 1941 (extermination operation from autumn of 1942 to July 24, 1944); (6) the extermination-industrial complex of Auschwitz (May 20, 1941–Jan. 27, 1945) where mass murder began in March 1942, and including Birkenau (Auschwitz II), with its extensive gas installations and crematoria (Nov. 26, 1941–Jan. 27, 1945), where extermination was going on from Nov. 26, 1941, to Dec. 1, 1944.

Auschwitz, in its extermination functions, was a multipurpose camp for the execution of Poles in general and Polish hostages in particular; physical destruction of sick and debilitated inmates—particularly Jews—shipped from various other camps, known as *Muselmanns* in the concentration camp slang; and medical experiments. However, it was primarily the site of the destruction of countless Jews transported there, gassed either immediately upon arrival or after a period of debilitating work in the widespread military industry.

The Jews constituted the lowest level of inmate in the camps. Jews were not considered human beings, but vermin, carriers of germs and diseases. They were constantly exposed to harassment and ill-treatment. Their lives were in perpetual danger. The same level of treatment existed for Jews who were detained in the concentration camps of the Reich proper during the war (see chap. 3). The camps were charged with a new mission in that period: the physical elimination of "undesirables" through medical-biological "experiments," mostly by injection of phenol. The victims of these "experiments," which, in fact, were murders known under the code name 14f13, were mental patients, invalids, and Jews. On Nov. 5, 1942, however, the Jews in the Reich camps were shipped to Auschwitz and Lublin under Heinrich Mueller's orders. The Austrian camp Mauthausen also served as an extermination center for Jews for a considerable period, as did the Prussian camp Stutthof, which absorbed large numbers of Eastern European Jews driven to the camp by the retreating Germans, who died there.

Methods of Psychological Warfare to Conceal Mass Murder. In implementing the Final Solution, including the deportations to the death camps, the Nazis ruthlessly used terror and various methods of psychological warfare. Random shooting was the order of the day in the collection centers. The Nazis were as deceitful in their conduct toward the victims, their relatives, and their leaders as they had been in their general strategy of concealing the extermination program and all traces of their crimes from the public.

The deliberate deception started with the first news of impending deportation which leaked into the ghetto, and did not end even at the entry to the gas chambers. Upon arrival in the extermination camp, the victims could detect no visible signs of the forthcoming disaster. The chambers were camouflaged and the entry was made to look like a disinfection shower. When ghetto inmates, by some acute sense of anticipation, learned of the imminent deportations and of the fate of the deportees, they appealed to their 35 leaders. The latter, turning to the Nazi authorities, received nothing but brazenly and forcefully expressed denials, along with threats of investigation of "mischief." When Jews were collected for deportation, they were told that they were being sent, e.g., for agricultural labor in the Ukraine, that this was the first and last deportation, and that the remaining Jews would continue their "normal life." Railway personnel reported to deportees' relatives about their "good life" in new places and undertook to transmit money and letters to them. In the heat of the deportations the Nazi authorities in the General Government issued orders for the establishment of new ghettos to strengthen the illusion of the forthcoming return from the East. Deportees from Hungary to Auschwitz were made to write to their relatives that they were in Waldsee, a summer resort in Austria.

CONCENTRATION CAMPS FOR THE REMNANTS OF THE LIQUIDATED GHETTOS. The year 1943 saw the end of the

Transport of women and children arrives at Auschwitz. Courtesy
Yad Vashem Archives, Jerusalem.

destruction of Polish Jewry under the code name *Aktion Reinhard* (from 1942 to November 1943) and of extermination activities in the Occupied Eastern Territories (German-annexed areas of western Poland). The survivors of these operations were mostly liquidated in *Restghettos* (residual ghettos) which were emptied one after another. Four extermination camps were also closed (one of them, Belzec, was later reactivated), and on Nov. 26, 1944, Himmler ordered an end to gassing. The miserable remnants were Jews still able to work *(Arbeitsjuden),* who were *"kaserniert"* (i.e., detained under separation of sexes) in a small number of concentration camps under the S.S.-W.V.H.A. They worked in the newly established S.S. Industrial Corporation Osti *(Ostindustrie)* or under the Armaments Inspection, the supervisory organ for the army industries. With the accelerated Soviet march toward the West, the final stage of *Aktion Reinhard* took place. The remaining Jews were either exterminated on the spot (as,

Children of Lodz are taken to extermination camp. 1942. Courtesy Yad Vashem Archives, Jerusalem.

e.g., operation "harvest home"—*Aktion Erntefest*—in the concentration camps of Majdanek, Trawniki, and Poniatowa) or shipped to various concentration camps in Germany, where conditions were as inhuman as in the camps in the East. Survivors of the chaotic conditions in the camps, and of the death marches (January–May 1945), were liberated by the Soviets and the Western Allies, and constituted the nucleus of the Displaced Persons in Germany, Austria, and Italy.

GERMAN CHURCHES AND THE HOLOCAUST. Despite the secrecy, the truth, even if not the whole truth, about the physical destruction of millions of Jews, known to certain party and government officials quite early, gradually spread all over Germany, mainly through military men on leave. The fact that a pastoral letter of Catholic bishops on Aug. 19, 1943, condemned "murder of innocent people" (although without direct mention of Jews), and the Confessing Church (the anti-Nazi *Bekenntniskirche*) did the same two months later (with explicit mention of "race" being no justification for murder) indicates that in the second half of 1943 the knowledge of mass murder was widespread. This reaction of the churches can be characterized as mild, vague, and belated. It is, however, significant that the deportation of the Jews from Germany which was going on for years did not elicit any protest action from the churches.

CHURCHES OUTSIDE GERMANY. The attitude of the churches outside Germany was not uniform. The Greek Orthodox Church of the Soviet Union (active in wartime) did not even enter a claim to rescue Jews, whereas the Bulgarian Greek Orthodox Church denied the government the right to persecute Jews on the grounds that "the fate of the latter is in the hands of God, not men." The same church in Rumania, although anti-Semitic, opposed the deportation and slaughter of the Jews. The Metropolitan of the Ukrainian Uniate Church in Lvov, Andreas Szeptycki, in a pastoral letter of July 1, 1941, expressed the expectation that the newly established Ukrainian government would care for the needs of all citizens "without discrimination on reasons of religion and nationality." In the following years (1942 and 1943) he openly condemned mass murder of Jews and was active in rescuing operations. In Athens Archbishop S. B. Damaskinos headed a group of 29 organizations that petitioned the prime minister to stop the deportation from Salonika. Protestant churches in Allied countries were outspoken in their protest. In the Roman Catholic Church, the local hierarchy and the Vatican nuncios in certain capitals (e.g., Monsignor Angelo Roncalli in Istanbul, later Pope John XXIII; Monsignor Andrea Cassulo in Bucharest; Monsignor Angelo Rotta in Budapest; and Monsignor Guiseppe Barzio in Bratislava) displayed more activity in rescue efforts than did the Vatican (see chap. 7).

THE LOCAL POPULATION AND THE HOLOCAUST. The attitudes of local populations toward their Jewish neighbors ranged from active sympathy (expressed in efforts to rescue Jews), through apathy, to direct hostility (culminating in betrayal of hidden Jews and direct participation in individual and group executions). These attitudes varied in different areas (as between East and West Europe), at different times in the same areas, and in different groups of population. Many factors were involved: the attitude of the Nazi or pro-Nazi regimes; the advice given by the governments-in-exile to the population in occupied territories, or by political opposition in Germany and in the satellites; and the risks involved in sheltering Jews. Not to be overlooked is the temptation to get hold of Jewish property or simply to be generously paid for rescuing Jewish lives. The risks varied in particular areas from the threat of the death penalty (in the General Government), to detention in a concentration camp that sometimes lasted through the entire occupation period (in the Netherlands). The risks were also different for various categories of Jews. There were less risks, e.g., in "Aryans" hiding "Aryan-looking" Jews, or persons whose pronunciation did not betray their "race," or persons who had "Aryan" friends. There is every reason to believe that, *ceteris paribus,* these risks had a decisive influence on the attitude of the local population.

With the exception of the Polish-Soviet area, the extent of indigenous anti-Semitism generally had no bearing on the number of victims. Outstanding examples are the Netherlands and Serbia, areas of no, or insignificant, anti-Jewish feeling but of high rates of losses, and Rumania, for decades anti-Semitic but with a relatively low rate of losses. However, friendly relations between Jews and non-Jews could prove a powerful rescue factor: the massive and effective rescue operation of Denmark's Jews brought to Sweden by sea, organized by the local Danish Resistance movement in October 1943; the widely observed protest strike in Amsterdam on Feb. 25 and 26, 1941, initiated by the Communist Party as a show of sympathy against the deportation two days earlier of some 400 Jews to Buchenwald and then to Mauthausen—the only strike of this sort in all of Europe; and the efforts of tens of thousands of Dutch people to give help to the persecuted Jewish population over the years. These examples stand out during the entire period of persecution and extermination. Not to be overlooked are the " righteous of the Nations" all over Europe who, out of sheer humanity, rescued Jews.

THE INTERNATIONAL RED CROSS. The International Red Cross (IRC) considered itself lacking in legal authority to deal with the Jewish situation in Hitler's Europe. It was totally banned by the Nazi government from the Polish-Soviet and "Great German" areas, except in June 1944 when its emissaries were admitted to Theresienstadt, and a second time in April 1945, on the eve of the Soviet army's entry. The activities of the IRC emissaries in Rumania, however, and their visits to Transnistria in 1943, played a role in the rescue of Rumanian Jews. The IRC did ship food and medicine through the Mixed Relief Commission of the IRC to Theresienstadt, Croatia, France, the Netherlands, Italy, Latvia, Poland, Slovakia, and Slovenia. In Auschwitz, IRC representatives witnessed the dissolution of the camp. During the period of the collapse of the Reich, the IRC was allowed to render some help to the Nazi victims in Germany.

THE JEWISH SOCIETY IN EXTREMIS. In the non-Communist East European countries and in other regions affected by the Nazi onslaught, the Jews were as different in their religious practice, moral and intellectual standards, occupations, and political affiliations as any social group can be. On the one hand they lacked the inner cohesion which had given strength to pre-emancipatory Judaism, and on the other they had not developed new forms of common ethos which might have been a factor in dealing with an enemy who was ruthless and equipped with the machinery of modern technology, communication, and organization. In the new compulsory and heterogenous "community·life" imposed by the enemy, such factors as individualism, party affiliations, and religion were inadequate as instruments of positive common ideology and action.

Those who had assimilated or converted to Christianity were torn between the slowly vanishing illusions that the efforts of generations of being "like all the gentiles" had engendered in them, and the growing awareness of "being different," which was rekindled when they were thrown together with the masses of Jewish-conscious Jews. At the other extreme were the Orthodox Jews, who in non-Soviet Eastern Europe constituted about half of the total Jewish population. They could not convincingly explain the Nazi persecution as a penalty for their sins, and were helpless in the face of the agonizing theological question: How could God allow this to happen? The majority of the Orthodox could not but realize that the traditional Jewish way of life had suffered a mortal blow, and some rabbis encouraged the belief that life was to be preserved at all cost, even through violation of the Law. Those who said "We shall serve the Holy One, blessed be He, despite everything He does to destroy our faith in Him" were confronted by the disciples of Rabbi Levi Isaac of Berdichev[4] who, in an earlier period, summoned the Holy One, blessed be He, to litigation, as it were, asking, "Why hast Thou chosen us to be the victims?"

[4] Famous ḥasidic ẓaddik and rabbi (c. 1740–1810)

For the actively Jewish secular sector, whose major groups were the socialists of various shades and the different Zionist organizations, to belong to the democratic Socialist International, previously an element of strength in the fight against "classic" anti-Semitism, was no source of aid. No effective help was forthcoming from members of the International during the Nazi period—neither from the socialist leaders in exile nor from socialist partners in some governments-in-exile. Jewish Communists, having great difficulty in accepting Moscow's characterization of the Nazis as "lovers of peace" prior to the invasion of the U.S.S.R., painfully returned to the Jewish fold after the invasion of the U.S.S.R. Resentment toward them by other parties was intensified when the Soviet authorities murdered Jewish Socialist leaders (December 1941). The Zionists were in dismay at the Mandatory power's restriction on immigration to Palestine at a time when this restriction meant death for countless human beings, and eventually the devastation of the potential reservoir of future emigration.

There were, however, two things which the converted, the assimilated, the religious, and the secular Jews had in common. Unlike the German prisoners of war in the U.S.S.R., some of whom felt that their treatment was still better than that accorded to Soviet prisoners by their own countrymen and thus had reason to resign themselves to their situation as a deserved punishment, no such reaction could occur among Jewish victims. Moreover, unlike the political detainees in Nazi concentration camps or the political prisoners in Stalinist camps, who for the most part could comprehend their detention and their sufferings as a consequence of their fight against their persecutors and could thus hope to summon psychological powers of resistance, the Jewish victims lacked a positive moral force, and as a result they were more easily prone to pessimism and hopelessness. At the same time, however, the mystical belief that Hitler would ultimately be defeated was widespread. The second common characteristic of all the

Jewish victims was the age-old strength of Jewish family ties, which under the Nazis unfortunately worked against them: breaking up the family might have afforded a better chance of rescue, but it would have destroyed the moral fabric of the members of the family. A loss in the family frequently paralyzed the other members and often reduced the general physical and mental stamina of those who remained alive.

JEWISH ATTITUDES. The attitudes of the Jewish victims toward the Nazi terror varied with their ages, political affiliations, religious convictions, and opportunities of avoiding the terror. The elements of Jewish existence were fundamentally different from those of their non-Jewish neighbors, namely: isolation from the outside world; the absence of the possibility to continue normal economic activities; detention of large masses in ghettos and Jewish quarters; obstacles to hiding because of high degree of Jewish recognizability by type and circumcision; strong family ties which frequently jeopardized the family as a whole; the reluctance of non-Jews to be identified as Jewish sympathizers; no government-in-exile allied with the anti-Axis coalition; and difficulties in communicating with other Jewish communities, and especially those in the free world.

Roughly speaking, the victims fall into two categories: those gradually conditioned by various inhuman methods to a loss of their physical and mental powers of resistance (e.g., in the Polish areas), and those surprised by sudden attack (e.g., in the U.S.S.R. and Serbia). In polarized categories they are frequently characterized as *heroica* and martyrdom *(kiddush ha-Shem)*. The *heroica* embrace resistance in all its manifestations: attempts at evading Nazi terror by forged documents ("Aryan papers"); procuring foreign passports ("legally" and "illegally"); attempts at circumventing the Nazi orders which imposed restrictions affecting daily life along with ingenious devices intended to halt, or slow down, the Nazi policy of starvation and emaciation; attempts at preserving Jewish life by all possible "illegal" means, including bribing Nazis; spiritual 43 resistance, to preserve human dignity in the face of Nazi terror, including the establishment and maintenance of "illegal" educational institutions on all levels, and preserving records of the Holocaust for future generations; participation in armed resistance movements, and creation of Jewish armed groups, which involved difficulties and dangers both from the Nazis and fellow partisans; the ghetto fighters who fought for Jewish honor without any hope of survival manifested in the Warsaw ghetto uprising; and the acts of armed resistance in the extermination camp of Auschwitz and outright revolt in Treblinka and Sobibor. The dangerous flights of Jewish inmates from extermination camps was a form of resistance that brought the story of the slaughter of a people before the world. Decorations for bravery given to Jewish members of the Allied armies and partisans were disproportionally numerous, due to a large extent to their realization that they fought an enemy not only of their country, but also of their own people. This applies even more so to the Palestinian Jewish Brigade and the Haganah parachutists from Palestine, among whom were Enzo Sereni and Hannah Szenes.

JEWISH COUNCILS (JUDENRAT). With the elimination of the Jews from the administrative apparatus of society at large, the creation of some form of Jewish administration was a vital necessity. Indeed, in many places, such as Warsaw and Lublin, the activities of the *kehillah* (community) were renewed even before Nazi initiative.

Extending their policy of Jews administering their own affairs under the supervision of the Gestapo in the "Greater German Reich," the Nazis planned to use the tradition of Jewish community organization for their own purposes in the occupied areas too. The Jews were to administer their communities and ghettos by implementing the Nazi orders. Simultaneously, the councils assumed responsibility on their own initiative for the welfare, economic life, and education of the communities.

The degree of influence and supervision by the Nazi authorities over the councils of Germany gradually but consistently increased, forming a long tortuous road from the Jewish-initiated Reichsvertretung to the Nazi-imposed Reichsvereingung. On the other hand, the Kultusgemeinde in Vienna and Prague, and the Aeltestenrat in Theresienstadt were under strong Gestapo pressure from the start. In Western Europe the parallel Nazi-sponsored institutions were the Joodse Raad voor Amsterdam, with jurisdiction over all of the Netherlands, and the Association des Juifs en Belgique. The Jewish administrations in the satellites were the locally imposed but Nazi-directed Ústredňa Židov in Slovakia, the ineffective Rumanian-created Centrala Evreilor din România, the Nazi-initiated Magyar Zsidók Központi Tanścsa in Hungary, and a Nazi-appointed president of the Salonika Jewish community. A special place was occupied by the French-imposed, but German-inspired Union Générale des Israélites de France (UGIF), and the Ústredňa Židov in the last deportation from Slovakia.

All of the above institutions were central for the specific regions. Not so in Eastern Europe where the activities of directly Nazi-controlled local and county Jewish councils were regulated by various Nazi orders and ordinances and, above all, by the arbitrary rule of the local Nazi polyarchy. The latter consisted of ghetto commissars and ghetto administration; S.D. and S.S.; higher, middle, and lower echelons of the Nazi administration; and to some extent the indigenous municipal administration.

The functions of all these councils were partly in the interests of the Jews, and partly in the Nazi interest. They were institutions of cooperation, but not necessarily collaboration, with the Nazis.

The overwhelming majority of those called upon to assume the functions of members of the Judenrat did so out of the traditional sense of Jewish communal responsibility. They became gradually apprehensive of the dangers inherent in this office, as exemplified in two dicta contained in secret Nazi documents referring to the General Government, but undoubtedly of general application: (1) "The 45

Die Strafe

Two drawings from a series depicting daily existence in a concentration camp, by a young girl from Berlin, Ella Lieberman, who lived through the horrors of Polish ghettos, Auschwitz, and Ravensbrueck. The drawings were made from memory after her liberation in May 1945. She later settled in Israel. Courtesy Yad Vashem Archives, Jerusalem.

Das Bad

Judenrat is to be made fully responsible *(vollverantwortlich)* in the precise meaning of the word for the implementation according to schedule *(terminmaessige Ausfuehrung)* of all directives, present and future" (Heydrich's instructions to the *Einsatzgruppen,* Sept. 21, 1939); and (2) "Whenever difficulties arise, the dissatisfaction of the Jews is directed against the Jewish administration and not against the German supervisory organs" (Warsaw Ghetto Commissar Heinz Auerswald in a letter to von Medazza, Hans Frank's representative in Berlin, Nov. 24, 1941). The Judenrat, therefore, served as a hostage group for the "good behavior" of the communities and as a lightning rod for Nazi misdeeds.

The process by which the members of the councils became gradually more and more submissive has been strikingly formulated by Rezső Kasztner[5]: "Step by step they were made tractable. In the beginning relatively unimportant things were asked of them, replaceable things of material value like personal possessions, money, and apartments. Later, however, the personal freedom of the human being was demanded. Finally, the Nazis asked for life itself" *(Report,* p. 67). This gradualism in demands, coupled with ever-increasing terror, was an ingenious and effective psychological device.

It is difficult to imagine that the ghettoized masses could have physically existed at all without the presence of the Jewish councils. Whether sympathetic or unsympathetic, or even opposed to the resistance, the councils contributed directly or indirectly to the resistance movements by their very presence. In the Eastern areas the *résistants* infiltrated some council organizations, using council-issued identification and police cards. In the last phase of its existence the Ústredňa Židov in Slovakia became an organ of resistance and rescue for all of Europe.

The crisis came when and where the Judenrat was called upon to assist in deportations to the death camps, particularly after the destination of the deportees was

[5] Zionist leader in Rumania and Hungary

already known. In the meantime the original composition of the Jewish councils had changed considerably, with a lowering in the level of character, judgment, and ability of members. Some of the members committed suicide or refused to cooperate and were repressed. The majority continued in office. There is no evidence that where there were no Jewish councils (e.g., in the first phase of the German invasion of the U.S.S.R.), or where their help was not solicited (as, e.g., Union Générale des Israélites de France), the percentage of losses were lower due to the lack of "assistance." Nor were the Nazis impressed by the supreme self-sacrifice of Adam Czerniakow, chairman of the Warsaw Jewish Council, who committed suicide on learning of the forthcoming deportation of Warsaw' Jews for extermination. Further, there is no evidence that the replacement of members of councils less inclined to "cooperate" by those more inclined to do so (as, e.g., the replacement of Artur Rosenzweig by David Guter in Cracow) had any influence on the final outcome. The special privileges accorded by the Nazis to council members notwithstanding, the percentage of victims among the members of the Jewish councils was practically the same as that of their constituencies. In the final analysis, the Nazis had sufficient time to complete their task with or without the Jewish councils, witnessed by the fact that the process of destruction of the Jews was practically completed long before the end of the war, or even before Himmler's order to stop the extermination.

JEWISH POLICE. Internal order within the ghettos was maintained by the Ordnungsdienst recruited among the Jewish population (Jewish police). The Jewish police constituted the executive arm of the Judenrat. The police was drawn from lower economic strata than the members of the Judenrat and were less educated, although originally some people with academic education volunteered to join the police ranks as a service, without salary. The majority had no background in Jewish communal organization. The motivation for joining the force ranged from an honest 49 desire to help the community, to base acquisitive aspiration. While the policemen enjoyed certain privileges, such as exemption from forced labor duty, larger food allocations, and postponement of resettlement, they received no pay in Warsaw and some other places. This factor accounts, perhaps, for the unwillingness of some to join the force, although it was, in fact, interpreted as a direct invitation to the recruit to make money in his own way: corruption at the expense of the ghetto inmates was rampant. Further demoralizing factors were Nazi plants in the ranks of the police and, in some larger ghettos, underworld penetration into the force. Not to be ignored was the demoralizing influence of daily contact between the Jewish policemen and their Nazi masters. Ultimately, the Jewish police shared the fate of all Jews.

THE LIBERATION OF EUROPE AND THE JEWISH SITUATION. The victorious march of the anti-Axis coalition from the East and West, following the German capitulation at Stalingrad, Allied successes in Africa, and Italy's surrender to the Allies, was, unlike the subjugation of Europe by the Nazis and their allies, a gradual and protracted process. One of the factors involved was the conflicting strategic plans of the United Nations ignoring implications for the fate of the Jews, "the anonymous ally." Along with the armies, the United Nations Relief and Rehabilitation Agency (UNRRA), established Nov. 9, 1943, was active in the liberated areas in "helping the people to help themselves" (its first director general Herbert Lehman[6]).

For the Jews, however, the aftermath of the Holocaust was a painful one. In the liberated areas, including Germany, the remnants of the Jewish population were in essence a mass of homeless and uprooted people, robbed of all material goods, undernourished and undermined in health. Emerging from the barbed wire of labor and concentration camps, they were haunted by nightmares of horrors experienced or witnessed—of gas chambers, long ditches filled with bodies, the S.S. dogs, the

[6] U.S. leader: former governor: later senator

piles of women's hair, suitcases with gold teeth, fertilizers from the factories of death. Some also emerged after years of hiding or of leading a guerilla life. The survivors were mostly without families, and without loyalties to their native countries, but with a strengthened attachment to their own people and its aspirations—especially the hope to establish a Jewish State in Palestine. Their willingness to face hardships in order to reach Palestine was dramatically expressed by Displaced Persons' representatives to a UN subcommittee on the future government of Palestine. Nor did victory of the Allies prove to be a panacea against indigeneous anti-Semitism buttressed by the conflicting interests of the Jewish survivors and those who had taken over their property, homes, and businesses. All this made repatriation in Eastern Europe practically impossible. The outstanding post-Holocaust feature, consequently, was the renewal of Jewish mass wandering inter alia, from the U.S.S.R. to Poland and from there, along with Jewish survivors in Poland, to the DPs camps in Germany, Austria, and Italy. They were joined by some 50,000 DPs who had been found by the liberating forces in Germany's concentration camps. Their numbers consequently swelled through spontaneous and partly organized flights (Beriḥah) to some 250,000 because of the hostility of the local Polish population, especially after the Kielce pogrom.[7] It took years before these camps were gradually evacuated by emigration, mostly to Israel and the U.S.

Among the problems that faced the survivors, and Jews everywhere, was that of meting out justice to the Nazis and their accomplices. The suicides of Hitler, Himmler, Goebbels, and later Goering, following his death sentence; the Nuremberg war trials (see below chap. 8), in which the defendants included such "murderers behind the desk" as Alfred Rosenberg and Julius Streicher and numerous others responsible for the Holocaust; and many other trials, including the Eichmann trial in Jerusalem, were received

[7] Pogrom in 1946 when 46 survivors of the Holocaust were killed by a Polish mob.

with satisfaction in the anti-Nazi world. While the promises of restitution and compensation contained in the peace treaties of the Allies with former Nazi satellites in Eastern Europe remained paper promises, Germany concluded a separate "reparation agreement" with Israel in 1952 and enacted restitution and compensation legislation.

NUMBER OF VICTIMS. The simplest method of arriving at the number of victims through direct or indirect murder (including suicides) would be to add up the figures appearing in individual reports on victims in ghettos, labor camps, extermination camps, and specific *Aktionen* by the Nazis and their accomplices. However, insofar as such Nazi reports on losses are available, they refer only to a fraction of the totality of *Aktionen,* and therefore this method is inapplicable. Exact statistics exist for deportations to death camps from Germany, France, Belgium, the Netherlands, and Theresienstadt, but not from other areas. The reports of the *Einsatzgruppen* on Jewish victims are far from complete. The extermination camps did not supply exact statistics of their victims. It is generally assumed that complete statistics were kept in Eichmann's office, but documentation there was deliberately destroyed. An available Nazi source is Richard Korherr's statistical report (complete version Nov. 9, 1943, *Geheime Reichssache. Die Endloesung der europaeischen Judenfrage*) but it does not go beyond Dec. 31, 1942, when the extermination process was still in full swing. Area-by-area statistics must therefore be used. Reliable estimates or exact numbers of total losses for the following large areas are known: Germany, Austria, Czechoslovakia, Hungary, France, Belgium, Luxembourg, Italy, the Netherlands, Norway, Rumania, Yugoslavia, and Greece. Difficulties arise in regard to Poland and the expanded U.S.S.R., due to migrations between these two areas, so that for statistical purposes they must be considered as one unit. There can be no doubt as to the estimated figure of some six million victims.

Auschwitz inmates who committed suicide by hurling themselves onto the high-voltage fence. Courtesy Yad Vashem Archives, Jerusalem.

Bergen Belsen. Corpses of inmates found by the British army when they liberated the camp. Courtesy Imperial War Museum, London.

Estimates of Jewish Victims During the Holocaust[1]

Polish-Soviet area[2]	4,565,000
Germany[3]	125,000
Austria[4]	65,000
Czechoslovakia (in the pre-Munich boundaries)[5]	277,000
Hungary, including northern Transylvania[6]	402,000
France[7]	83,000
Belgium[8]	24,000
Luxembourg[9]	700
Italy[10]	7,500
The Netherlands[11]	106,000
Norway[12]	760
Rumania (Regat, southern Transylvania, southern Bukovina)[13]	40,000
Yugoslavia[14]	60,000
Greece[15]	65,000
Total loss	**5,820,960**

[1] With few exceptions, there are no mathematically exact Jewish statistics in accordance with generally accepted scientific standards. Not even official censuses qualify for this distinction. With the exception of the Polish-Soviet area, the figures here refer to factual losses, which are much less than the Nazi-caused demographic deficit.

[2] This figure was arrived at by the following calculations: The Jewish population of the Polish area on the eve of the German invasion (Sept. 1, 1939) was 3,351,000 (Polish Ministry of Information, London, *Concise Statistical Yearbook of Poland, Sept. 1939 to June 1941*, p. 10).

In the U.S.S.R. (boundaries of Sept. 1, 1939) the census carried the round figure of 3,020,000 Jews plus an estimated natural increase in the period between the date of this census (Jan. 17, 1939) and that of the German invasion (June 22, 1941) of 80,000	3,100,000
in Lithuania	155,000
In Latvia	95,000
In Estonia	4,000
In Bessarabia and northern Bukovina, calculated on the basis of the 1930 Rumanian census of 278,000 plus minimal results of natural and mechanical population movement	300,000
Total Jewish population in the Polish-Soviet area, Sept. 1, 1939	7,005,000
Jewish population in the expanded U.S.S.R. in 1959: this figure also includes the former Carpatho-Ukraine, annexed to the U.S.S.R. after 1945, but with hardly any Jews left. The figure represents the number of Jews who declared themselves as such. The number of "hidden" Jews, a phenomenon as relevant to the 1939 as to the 1959 census, or the number of persons of mixed marriages (Jew-gentile) and how they registered in the census under the nationality category, is a matter of speculation	2,268,000

The growth of the Soviet population from the end of the war to the 1959 census was 25 percent; the growth of the Jewish population, estimated to be $\frac{1}{4}$ below the general percentage, should have been, by the end of the war

1,910,000

(S.M. Schwarz, *Jews in the Soviet Union 1939–1965* (1966), 171–2, notes 36–39 [Russian]).

This figure must be amended by the "repatriates" to Poland from the U.S.S.R. and survivors of this area in Poland, in the various DP camps, and scattered all over the globe

300,000

Total Jewish population in the area by the end of the war

2,210,000

Subtracting this figure from 7,005,000 leaves

4,795,000

The last figure represents the total demographic deficit of Jewry in the Polish-Soviet area. To calculate the deficit due to the Holocaust, one must subtract Jewish military casualties in the Polish Army

30,000

and estimated Jewish losses in the Red Army

200,000

Jewish Holocaust deficit

4,565,000

3 According to Bruno Blau (in *Jewish Social Studies*, April 1950, 161–72) there were some 118,000 Jewish victims of deportation in Germany during the period beginning May 1, 1941. To this figure some 7,000 more victims must be added: deportations prior to May 1, 1941 (from Stettin), and all other cases of violent death in Germany, particularly in German concentration camps. The round figure of 125,000 may be accepted as a minimal figure. Not included are German Jews who fled to European countries and were caught by the Nazis there (e.g., in Belgium, France, the Netherlands), and are included in the statistics of victims of those areas. The additional demographic deficit was 72,000 (H. Hoehne, *Der Orden unter dem Totenkopf*, 1966, 306).

4 Moser, in: *Widerstand, Verfolgung und Emigration*. Forschungsinstitut der Friedrich-Ebert-Stiftung (1967), 21–22.

5 Adler, in: *Algemeyne Entsiklopedye*, vol. 7, p. 90.

6 Roth, *ibid.*, p. 141 (297,000 in Trianon, Hungary). In northern Transylvania there were some 150,000 Jews (*ibid.*, p. 344), of whom 45,000 survived (*ibid.*, p. 141). Total loss, 105,000.

7 Calculated on the basis of the deportee lists (Lucien Steinberg, *Les autorités allemandes en France*, Paris. Census, 1966, p. 173).

8 Billig, in: *Algemeyne Entsiklopedye*, VII, p. 212.

9 Billig, *ibid.*, VII, p. 220.

10 Robinson, *And the Crooked Shall Be Made Straight*. New York (1965), p. 251.

11 Presser, in: *Algemeyne Entsiklopedye*, VII, p. 262.

12 Mendelson, *ibid.*, VII, p. 290.

13 Calculated on the basis of Matatias Carp, *Cartea Neagra*, vol. III, 41–42, and *Pinkas ha-Kehillot*, Rumania, vol. 1 (1969), pp. קצח—קצט. The figure of 40,000 does not include Rumanian and northern Bukovina Jews who perished either by the march of the *Einsatzgruppen* in the Ukraine or in Transnistria. Nor does it include the victims of northern Transylvania which are included in item Hungary.

14 Alcalay, in: *Algemeyne Entsiklopedye*, VII, p. 367.

15 M. Molho and J. Nehama, *Sho'at Yehudei Yavan* (1965), 222.

RESCUE POSSIBILITIES. In view of the terrifying losses, the question of opportunities to have rescued at least part of the victims is inevitably raised. The fact is that once war had engulfed Europe, people could have been rescued, and, in fact, small numbers were rescued from the Nazi extermination machine by: (1) Himmler's stopping the death mills, which occurred only in November 1944; (2) organizing mass rescue flights (Denmark); (3) granting Jews special status (Swedish and Swiss protective papers for Hungarian Jews); (4) joining resistance groups (the Maquis in France; partisans in the Polish-Soviet area). Individual escape was also occasionally possible from labor camps, death trains, even from death camps like Auschwitz, and, perhaps most surprisingly, for the few survivors of the uprisings in the death camps of Treblinka and Sobibor. The long-term consequences of bribing German officials were of no decisive importance.

The intelligence services of the Allies were well informed of the "events of the East," a euphemism for mass murder. Jewish sources were most active in disseminating information on the massacres going on, particularly in the Polish-Soviet area. Jews in free countries tried to prod their governments to action, but the general attitude of the Allies was influenced by certain Allied interests (e.g., the White Paper policy of the United Kingdom), and by the fear that by openly helping Jews they would play into the hands of Hitler's propaganda about a "Jewish war." Consequently, the Allies single-mindedly upheld the view that a general victory alone could save the Jews. Thus, while the synthetic rubber works seven kilometers from Birkenau was bombed in April 1944, and the town of Auschwitz three kilometers from Birkenau were bombed in July 1944, as well as the hospital and S.S. barracks in Birkenau some 15 yards from the extermination sites on Dec. 24, 1944, no action was ever undertaken against the unguarded camp installations easily recognizable by the smoking fires of the crematoria. World Jewry felt overwhelming frustration, shared by men of good will everywhere, expressed by the bishop of London, speaking in the House of Lords, as a "horrible sense of impotence." Actual rescue operations were undertaken by members of the Allies very late (President Roosevelt established the War Refugee Board on Jan. 22, 1944). In any event, for the victims of the Polish-Russian area, these activities were of no avail. The attitudes of neutral states toward admission of victims or intervention in their favor changed with the fortunes of war. The attitude of Spain was more ambivalent, it being a member of the anti-Comintern pact from Mar. 27, 1939.

MATERIAL LOSSES. A conservative estimate of Jewish material losses is 12 billion dollars at values of that time. Only a small part of the property was returned and only part of the damage caused by loss of life, health, liberty, and professions was compensated.

END OF A CIVILIZATION. The greatest loss of all is the loss of the Jewish civilization of Central, Eastern (Ashkenazi), and Southern (Salonika-Sephardi) Europe, not only in terms of numbers and material aspects, but in its rabbinical and secular creativity in Hebrew, Yiddish, and local languages. East European Jewry in particular, for centuries a reservoir of world Jewry, came to an abrupt end.

2 THE BEHAVIOR OF THE VICTIMS

WHO IS COMPETENT TO JUDGE THIS BEHAVIOR? A problem that has been hotly debated between survivors and out- siders has been: who is competent to describe and evaluate authoritatively the behavior of the victims and their leaders. Many survivors held the view that "no one who has not had any personal experience of a German concentration camp can possibly have the remotest concep- tion of concentration camp life." "Little does the outsider know of the hard fight for existence which raged among prisoners." Admittedly, they have the advantage of the immediate personal experience of a phenomenon not easily imaginable. But acceptance of this claim at its face value would mean that with the last survivor gone, research and evaluation of such behavior would also come to an end. Nor could the danger be ignored of generalization by survivors who sometimes on the basis of brief and local experience in a camp or in a ghetto, arrive at conclusions of broader applications. On the other hand, it is not beyond the capacities of a conscientious witness or student to acquire knowledge and understanding, and to arm himself with *Einfuehlungsvermoegen* which is the proper meaning of the talmudic saying, "Judge not thy neighbor until thou art come into his place," as formulated in modern terms by Victor Frankl[8]: "No man should judge unless he asks himself in absolute honesty whether in a similar situation he might not have done the same."

Any attempt to apply to the victims of the Holocaust or of comparable situations standards of behavior of a civilized society must fail. "Standards of normal society did

[8] Jewish Austrian psychiatrist

not obtain in the ghettos and concentration camps. Theft, egotism, lack of consideration for others, disregarding all laws, all this was prohibited in pre-concentration camp days; inside the concentration camp, however, it was normal." In these conditions, "there was neither the time nor the desire to consider moral issues. Every man was controlled by one thought only: how to keep himself alive." The admitted purpose of the Nazis in regard to the Jewish victim—as long as he was alive—was to reduce the homo sapiens to the category of a primitive creature with steadily decreasing needs which were finally reduced to craving for food ("two hundred grams of bread ruled over life"—Solzhenitsyn[9]; "general preoccupation with food"—Frankl; "I am hungry, I am cold; when I grow up I want to be a German, and then I shall no longer be hungry, and no longer be cold"—diary of a child in the Warsaw ghetto).

Concentration on material relating to the behavior of Jews alone is insufficient for any valid judgment. Some contemporary phenomena with a degree of comparability are certain to supply significant insights into the psychology of terrorized men, for example the behavior of political opponents in Nazi Germany and in the U.S.S.R., of Soviet and German prisoners of war during World War II, of detainees in Stalinist camps, and of defendants and onlookers in the 1936/37 Moscow trials.

MASS BEHAVIOR. The behavior of the masses will be discussed under the following headings: the invasion period: deportations inside prewar Poland; isolation-ghettos, labor camps and squads (inside and outside the ghettos); collection of deportees and deportation to the death camps; behavior in death camps.

Behavior During the Invasion. The inevitable concomitant of war is the flight of refugees from the area of hostilities. A survey of the behavior of the Jews in invaded Eastern and Western Europe shows the following picture:

[9] Russian writer who described his experiences in Russian labor camps under the Stalinist regime

from the start of the invasion on, in addition to non-Jews more than 300,000 Jews from Poland fled, in the conditions of a catastrophic military defeat and of the total collapse of state and government, to the Eastern non-Nazi-occupied Polish territories, which were occupied by the Soviet troops on Sept. 17, 1939, and further east; to the Vilna region (temporarily occupied by the Soviets, later transferred to Lithuania); to the southern part of Lithuania; and to Rumania and Hungary. The Jews formed the majority of Polish refugees everywhere but in Rumania and Hungary. This movement came to a halt when all powers involved sealed off their boundaries. No significant flights were reported from Western Europe during the period of the "phoney war."

The stiuation changed with the beginning of hostilities when non-Jews and Jews from France, Belgium, and, to a lesser degree, from the Netherlands used all available roads and vehicles to escape the invading armies. After the beginning of German-Soviet hostilities no such spontaneous movement of Jews was reported from the U.S.S.R. in her prewar boundaries because of the suddenness of the invasion and the psychological unpreparedness of the Jewish population, and also because of the Soviet press's complete silence concerning Nazi persecution of Jews in Poland during the period of the Soviet alliance with Nazi Germany. Similarly, the suddenness of the invasion of Yugoslavia made any large movement of Jewish refugees practically impossible. On the other hand Jews were among the beneficiaries of the government-sponsored evacuation of special categories of state and party officials and industry personnel.

Prewar Behavior During the Deportations Inside Poland.
The break-up of the German-occupied part of Poland into the General Government and the Incorporated Eastern Territories and Western areas annexed to the Reich had one dire consequence for some 100,000 Jews and 200,000 Poles of the latter areas; they were to be swiftly

depolonized and dejudaized, and subjected to mass deportations, with all that this implied. The evidence is that Poles and Jews alike, stunned by the debacle and utterly not comprehending the meaning of German deportation orders, met their fate without any external sign of resistance.

Behavior of Jews in Isolation. The specificity of the Jewish behavior begins with the next stage of persecution, namely, isolation, which was carried out consistently in the east, partially in the south, and—if at all, in a different setting—in the west of Europe. No resistance was possible in the course of ghettoization, and in some respects, ghettoization was even desirable as a sort of defense against bloody pogroms, both spontaneous and Nazi-incited. Work in labor camps, an important factor in the gradual physical emaciation of the masses, had sometimes the disproportionate advantage of coming in touch with the gentile population, thus enabling the Jews to trade personal belongings for food. Numerous cases have been recorded where ghetto Jews, because of this possibility, even volunteered for outside labor. The same phenomenon was observed in the Soviet prisoners-of-war camps in the occupied areas. Only a few cases of sabotage by Jewish forced laborers were recorded, but they were not overly productive in their work under the slogan "work slowly." As to the masses enclosed in the ghettos, their basic if not exclusive desire was to rescue themselves and their families, ready to pay for it with suffering and humiliation for the sake of some faint hope of survival. They fought starvation and epidemics by making themselves useful as a skilled and unskilled labor force, creating new industries out of nothing, engaging in smuggling whenever it was possible. For example, in the ghetto of Warsaw, which had a Jewish population larger than that of all of continental Western Europe put together, and in other ghettos with lines of communications to the outside world, smuggling assumed gigantic proportions and flourished to the benefit of the inmates. "Perhaps, the day will come and the 61

Youngsters

Photographs taken in the Warsaw ghetto by a German war
correspondent. Oct. 1, 1940–June 1, 1941. Courtesy Yad
Vashem Archives, Jerusalem.

Old man

Jewish people will erect monuments to the unknown smugglers."

There are some records of spontaneous mass flights of Jews to the woods from the ghettos (after burning their houses), and of betrayals by the local population (e.g., Tulczyn). There are also known individual cases of disobedience to the orders of the Jewish councils (Judenrat) and of the police (e.g., evasion of labor duty or of the payment of fees for release from that duty, non-payment of taxes) and even physical resistance against certain actions of the Jewish police occurred in some ghettos. Hunger strikes and street demonstrations in the large Lodz ghetto are recorded, prompted mostly by labor and food conditions.

There was no lack of channels for the masses to express their dissatisfaction with their fate. In the General Government, the "Jewish Social Self-Help" organization (financed by the American Jewish Joint Distribution Committee), and in Warsaw the house committees, served this purpose. The party ties from the prewar time served not only to maintain—as far as possible—close relations between like-minded persons but were also a source of mutual help (party kitchens). The parties were also responsible for the widely distributed underground press—an·indispensable source of information. The ghetto dwellers established clandestine schools and prayer houses and tried to preserve the records of the Holocaust.

Demoralization of individual Jews had gone far enough in ghettos and outside the ghettos. The lowest depths of the first category was reached in Warsaw by a group of Jews on Dzika Street 13, called *Di Draytsentl,* who joined the Gestapo to oppress their fellow Jews (some of them were liquidated by the resistance movement), or in the activities of the Salonika collaborators (some of whom were sentenced to death by Greek courts and executed). In Amsterdam and Berlin (but not on the Aryan side of Warsaw) the height of demoralization was reached when some Jews betrayed their fellow Jews in hiding to the Nazi authorities. They, too, were later to answer for their crimes before state courts.

Behavior During Collection of the Deportees and Deportation to the Death Camps. No uniform picture of mass behavior emerges from the existing documentation. Attempts to evade "collection" and thus to escape deportation are registered practically everywhere. There was, however, an immense difference between the situation in areas of Jewish confinement (ghettos and transit camps) and areas where the Jews were not concentrated in particular places. Having received a summons to appear for *Arbeitseinsatz* (code name for the deportation in the Netherlands), Jews in the latter still had some chance to escape deportation. While large numbers of those who received summonses used to show up (prodded sometimes, in the case of the Netherlands, by members of the Jewish council, the Joodse Raad), others went into hiding with non-Jews, and a few refused to go into hiding as an act endangering non-Jews on the theory that Jews should not impose on non-Jews dangers meant for them only. The opportunities for hiding depended on the degree to which gentiles were willing to accept Jews, and on the sanctions imposed by the Germans for such assistance. There was no certainty in this attempt to escape; betrayal of the "submerged" was a daily occurrence.

Two distinguished writers have recorded instances of such behavior. A picture of Ukrainian peasants awaiting shipment to Germany for forced labor at a time when the local population was already well aware of conditions of life there is offered by Anatoly Kuznetsov[10] (*Babi Yar*, 286-7):

> I . . . tramped obediently into a yard behind one of the cottages. About fifteen peasants were there, old men and boys, some sitting on the mound around the cottage and others just on the ground. Their faces were passive, indifferent, empty of expression. Just to make sure, I asked a boy of my age, "Are they taking us to Germany?" "Uh-huh," he sniffled. "They are taking everybody." The raid was a quiet one. The soldiers went from cottage to cottage, hauling people out:

[10] Russian writer who wrote a novel about Babi Yar, where the Jews of Kiev were massacred by the Germans

64

the men came submissively, silently, just as I had come . . .
We were driven to a collective farm yard . . . Our few guards
were evidently so used to obedience from people that they
did not come into the yard with us . . . They [the peasants]
were all gray and ragged, and they sat in silence, in a dull
stupor.

The following is a striking description by the Polish
writer Ferdynand Goetel (*Czasy wojny,* 112) of the behavior
of the Jews in the small town of Zawichost, near Sando-
mierz:

"In the summer of 1943, a Gestapo squad arrived in Zawichost, called in the Jewish leaders *(starszyzna)* and announced
that in a few days the Jews would have to leave town. They
should be ready to march and await the arrival of the escort.
This happened at a time when Jews even in remote provinces
had no illusions as to what was in store for them . . . The
whole [Jewish] population of the town was on the spot . . .
looking at the road by which the German police was supposed
to arrive."

The author asked his companion (a local landlord): "Do they
know what is in store for them?" The companion: "Surely."
The author: "Why do they not disperse, why do they not escape?" The companion: "Where? To what place can they escape?"

As for the deportations themselves, the people were
locked in cattle cars with strong guards, not knowing their
destination and suspicious of the "final objective," subjected to fraud and deception by the Nazis. Here again there
were only individual cases of breaking out and jumping
from the moving trains, with all the dangers of such a
situation and the uncertainty of finding shelter with Polish
or Ukrainian people.

One must remember that for Polish Jews the moment of
collection and deportation came after 30 months of
unspeakable suffering that had reduced their power of
physical and mental resistance almost to zero. The
helplessness of collectees and deportees was due to the
generally shared unbelievability of the very idea of total
destruction of Jewish communities, the hopes that the
deportees, at least the men and women fit for work, were   65

being sent east to other camps or ghettos, and that the first selection would also be the last one. Perhaps the most striking proof of the strength of these illusions was the thousands of volunteers who crowded the *Umschlagplatz* (collection point) in Warsaw. The lack of an alternative (armed resistance in absence of weapons and difficulties of communication), fear of collective sanctions, messianic belief in Hitler's inevitable defeat—all created a sense of apathy. This analysis, borrowed from a thoughtful essay by the Polish-Jewish resistance fighter Adolf Berman written in January 1943, is *mutatis mutandis* applicable to other areas as well.

No escape at all was possible for the Jews in the expanded U.S.S.R. and in Yugoslavia, where—unlike Poland and Western Europe—the process of extermination started simultaneously with the invasion, at the hands of the *Einsatzgruppen* invested with unlimited authority to shoot hundreds of thousands of Jews and "communists." In the second wave of extermination (mostly by shooting) the behavior of the masses in those areas was analogous to that of the victims in the death camps in Poland. In the final wave of deportations (for example from Lithuania to Estonia), people were sent to labor.

Jewish Behavior in Death Camps. After the life in the ghettos and camps, after having lost the power of resistance under the constant Nazi terror, and often having also lost entire or part of their families, nothing but blind obedience could have been expected of these former persons when they were shipped to gas chambers which were disguised as showers. All thoughtful observers agree that in the death camps the normality of death "caused death to lose its terror." The calm that reigned among death candidates impressed various witnesses, some of them seeing it as a characteristic of dignified death in view of the impossibility to live a dignified life. The special commandos in the death camps were forced to perform the macabre job of sometimes accompanying (in Auschwitz) the victims to the gas chambers and, after their death, disposing of the corpses, extracting gold teeth, cutting hair, etc. In a later period, people of this category (when in Auschwitz they were threatened with physical destruction) or of the working groups in other camps took active parts in uprisings which occurred in Treblinka (Aug. 2, 1943), Sobibor (Oct. 14, 1943), and Chelmno (January 1945) at the cost of many Jewish lives as against the loss of only relatively few Nazi lives.

In the daily dilemma of the conflict between the instinctive will to remain alive at all cost and the faint hope of maintaining at least a certain amount of "God's image," the depth of human degradation for the condemned Jews was reached in the death camps. A look at comparable situations may be in order. In terms of numbers and ultimate fate, the Soviet prisoners of war came closest to the Jews, with two significant differences: they were young and mostly single and thus—among other things—spared the fate of having to witness the agony of their loved ones; and they were military men trained in the use of arms and indoctrinated with Soviet and Russian patriotism. Like the Jews, who were not protected by any international convention, these prisoners were also unprotected, since their government considered all of them as deserters and did not invoke the Geneva Convention on Prisoners of War. The remarks of a sympathetic observer, who spent some four months in three prisoners camps in Soviet-occupied areas with a capacity of 90,000 prisoners, have a familiar ring: "It was intolerable to realize that before the eyes of the whole civilized world millions of innocent people died a slow death."

Here are a few Dantesque scenes of their behavior:

The exhausted comrades were considered by the less exhausted ones as living corpses, and some of the stronger prisoners watched the dying and upon their death stripped them naked, sometimes even before they gasped their last breath. Despite cruel punishment meted out to marauders by their own comrades, these crimes continued, since in the climate of total demoralization punishment did not work. Groups of marauders—each with their own sphere of influence—acted collectively and with exclusive claim to the "property" of their victims. Another phenomenon in these camps was cannibalism. Corpses were found in the morning with hearts, livers, and large pieces from their insides cut out. The cannibals, if caught, were delivered to the Germans for death by shooting. And still it went on.

Under the circumstances, Jewish masses could not and did not—as a rule—revolt. No significant acts of sabotage or other forms of resistance have been recorded for their part by prisoners of war (both those internationally protected by the Geneva Convention and remaining mostly in camps in their home countries and—a fortiori—unprotected Soviet prisoners of war) or the millions (on Sept. 30, 1944—some $7\frac{1}{2}$ million) of European workers situated in the heart of Germany, many of them enjoying wide freedom of movement and other privileges or by non-Jewish prisoners of concentration camps (prior to 1945).

BEHAVIOR OF JEWISH OFFICIALS. *Jewish Councils (Judenraete).* Evaluation of the behavior of the members of the Jewish councils must be made in three areas: personal integrity, political acumen, and sense of responsibility for the community. No characterizations of a general nature can be made. The personal integrity of the members of the Joodse Raad in Amsterdam or of the Reichsvereinigung in Berlin was never questioned, in contrast to that of members of councils in Poland. Individual cases of misconduct on the part of some members of councils (e.g., extorting money from victims for better quarters) have been recorded. The political acumen of the average members in the daily conflict with the Machiavellian Nazis was not less than that of a Chamberlain or Daladier,[11] but not sufficient to avert disaster which visited the Jews no matter what they did. The sense of responsibility of members accepting the office is beyond question. A few examples out of many: Adam Czerniakow (Warsaw) was offered an immigration certificate for Palestine, but he refused to leave the community and eventually committed suicide. David

[11] British and French premiers who participated in the Munich agreement

Cohen (Amsterdam) received a visa to Switzerland but refused to leave. Julius Seligsohn (Berlin) returned from the U.S. to help in the Reichsvertretung and subsequently died in the concentration camp in Oranienburg.

The unsuccessful resistance to the ghettoization was fought by some Jewish officials not against the establishment of the "institution" as such but against the deadline for the "resettlement" and the geographic extent of the ghetto. No serious moral problems arose when the councils were requested to give the Germans what Kasztner called "replaceable things." The implementation of the forced labor duty by the Jewish councils, seen against the alternative of the Germans catching Jews on the streets at random and in view of the efforts of the councils to take care of the welfare of the laborers and their families, was still justifiable. For example, Shmuel Zygelbojm, then a member of the Warsaw Judenrat, referring to the above-mentioned "alternative" advised his colleagues: "We must tell the Germans that if they need labor they should turn to us and we will assign the necessary people." The release of well-to-do people from this duty for a certain amount paid to the treasury was not considered unjustifiable.

A critical test of the behavior of councils called upon to participate in the deportation to the death camps came at a time when the destination of the deportees became known. The question arising for the historian (behaviorist) is the following: Why did they not refuse to take the German orders when it was clear to them that they were becoming what is loosely called "accomplices of the Nazis"? Hope (sometimes materialized) for exemption from deportation of the Council member and his family and friends was built in in the four reasons which predominate in the contemporary literature:

(1) The Nazi terror against the recalcitrant members of the councils and their families and expected reprisals against the community for their acts and omissions. (2) The danger of refusal to cooperate would lead to the appointment of a new unscrupulous member (the principle of 69

negative selection). (3) The theory that alternatively no other person would be appointed to the Jewish council and the Germans would do the job themselves, with much more cruelty. (4) The hope that as long as selection remained in the hands of the Jewish leaders the best elements of the community may be preserved for its future rehabilitation.

This type of "cooperation" imposed by the Gestapo on the Berlin Jewish community in the process of "resettlement" was different. Under threats that otherwise the "S.S. and S.A. would do it alone," members of the *Gemeindevorstand* in Berlin were ordered to put at the disposal of the Gestapo its "register" of Berlin Jews. After a heated debate the Vorstand and the Reichsvereinigung agreed to cooperate "in the hope that they would be able to do as much as possible in the interests of the affected persons."

A special problem arose in cases in which councils, knowing the impending disaster, failed to share this knowledge with the people. Their behavior has been a subject of controversy. In places where nothing could have been done to change the course of events, it was considered by some members advisable not to let victims know the truth in order to spare them the agony and ultimate desperation that comes from knowing that the end is near and there is absolutely no way out. This was the policy followed, e.g., by Leo Baeck [12] in Theresienstadt when he saw that there was no possibility left to escape. On the other hand, such behavior provoked the charge of collaboration with the Nazis, who, too, tried to keep the destination of the victims secret.

The individual behavior of Council members varied all the way from participation in deportation to refusal, with the ensuing repression to suicide. Some, conscious of moral pangs, publicly vowed to appear after the war before a Jewish court to give account of their activities.

Fear of Nazi mass vengeance also was a factor in leading many council members to oppose resistance and flights from the ghettos to join the partisans, while others tolerated

[12] German rabbi, religious thinker, and German Jewish leader

or even encouraged such flights, and some were prepared to assume leadership for armed resistance or organized mass flights when, in their view, the proper moment came.

Canons of behavior in these extreme cases were formulated *post factum* by the Israel legislature and put to the test in Israel courts. Under Nazis and Nazi Collaborators (Punishment) Law 5710–1950, "the delivery of a persecuted person to an enemy administration" was declared a punishable crime (Art. 5 of the Law). The article covers all forms of participation in selection and deportation of Jews. The same law established two criteria for the release of a person from criminal responsibility: (1) if he did or omitted to do the act in order to save himself from the danger of immediate death threatening him and the court is satisfied that he did his best to avert the consequences of the act or omission, or (2) if he did or omitted to do the act with intent to avert consequences more serious than those which resulted from the act or omission, and actually averted them.

In the light of these canons the Israel courts were faced, among other things, with the following problems: (1) Are the criteria for legal evaluation of the acts of the Jewish participants in the deportation to be borrowed from normal codes of behavior in normal times or bearing in mind the particular nature of the Nazi period and the nature of an ordinary simple human being? (2) Is the non-resignation of a Jewish participant in deportation who had known the purpose of that deportation reprehensible? (3) Is the forced delivery of a minority of victims to the Nazis justified when proven that in such a case the immediate deportation of the majority was prevented? In other words, does such an act fall under the clause of "averting more serious consequences"? (4) Is the care for the Jewish participant's family and the threat to him and his family ground for releasing him from responsibility for this participation? It is difficult to say whether the Israel legislature's canons might have helped men of conscience to determine their decisions, had these canons been positive law in the ghettos.

From a traditionalist point of view, there was, however, the Code of Maimonides[13] (Yad, Hilkhot Yesodot ha-Torah, 5:5) under which "... if pagans should tell them [the Jews] 'give us one of yours and we shall kill him, otherwise we shall kill all of you,' they all should be killed and not a single Jewish soul should be delivered." However, the secular sector argued that the Code of Maimonides was obsolete and inapplicable. On the other hand the interpretations given to the Code of Maimonides even by rabbinical authorities were contradictory. Thus the rabbi of Kovno Abraham Duber Cahana Shapiro ruled that "if a Jewish community ... has been condemned to physical destruction, and there are means of rescuing part of it, the leaders of the community should have courage and assume the responsibility to act and rescue what is possible." In contrast, the Vilna rabbinate, replying to the argument of the head of the Judenrat that "by participating in the selections and delivering a small number of Jews, he is rescuing the rest from death" took the strict view of Maimonides.

Jewish Police. As in the case of Jewish councils, generalizations are of no help in analyzing the behavior of the police. As a general conclusion it may, however, be said, that in their conflicting duties toward the frequently non-Jewish commandants, the Jewish councils, the Nazi authorities, and their own community—there were considerable differences between large cities and small towns, where the relations of the police and the local Jews were close, as well as differences between local policemen and those recruited from among the refugees. The functions imposed on the Jewish police were, to say the least, distasteful: enforcement of obligatory labor duty and all this implies, in conditions where the evasion of one laborer was bought at the price of recruiting another one; collection of taxes and "contributions"; confiscations of Jewish property; combating smuggling (but also practicing it); participation in collecting deportees (mostly

72   [13] Medieval authority on Jewish law and philosophy

only in the first wave, a task later taken over entirely by the Germans), ranging from active search for hidden victims and their brutal treatment, particularly in the presence of Germans, through apathetic compliance with orders to clandestine help to the victims and even refusal to participate in the "hunt." The policemen and their families were promised exemption from resettlement in reward for participation in the collections and were threatened with reprisals for noncompliance. Naturally, the promises were not kept, the cadres of police were—after each "action"—reduced and the policemen and their families were also deported. Incidentally, there were differences of opinion among close observers of the scene whether participation of the Jewish police in the "actions" was not preferable to exclusive German participation.

The majority of police in areas without access to partisans opposed resistance. This policy was not unpopular among the masses who, fearing Nazi mass reprisal, likewise opposed resistance, while in the eastern (Polish-Soviet) areas cases of cooperation with assistance to *résistants* were rather frequent.

Perhaps the two extremes of the behavior of the Jewish policemen are epitomized in the ghettos of Warsaw and Kovno. The facts known about Warsaw (where, incidentally, a number of suicides and the evidence of an opposition group among policemen are recorded) differ in two respects from those in Kovno: police in the latter participated only perfunctorily in the collection of deportees while the former—with some exceptions—readily participated; and the Kovno police was in close contact with the *résistants* while no such contact is known in Warsaw (again with a few exceptions). The functions of Jewish supervisors in labor camps and *Kapos* in concentration camps were essentially police functions and offered to base persons opportunities for abuse and mistreatment of their charges.

The Soviet police in prisoner-of-war camps combined, so to say, the functions of the councils and the police. It consisted of healthy, strong, and amoral prisoners. These men

—with very few exceptions—knew no pity or compassion for their own comrades. They would beat up prisoners with impunity and frequently flog them to death. The black market of products "imported" to the camp was in their hands. They were the absolute masters of the camps.

Behavior of the Active Elite. The active elite consisted in the Polish and newly annexed Soviet area of representatives of party-affiliated and unaffiliated youth movements of various shades of opinion. It took some time to unite for a common cause groups that were ideologically opposed to each other, to overcome the reasoning of the older generation ("that was clinging to life while the young dreamed of death different from the one determined by the Nazis"), to create contact with the Polish underground, acquire from them arms, and use their channels of communication. These were exclusive groups reluctant to receive new members for reasons of security and the impossibility of sharing the pitiful supply of arms with newcomers.

The motivation of integrated Jewish participation in the resistance in Yugoslavia, the Netherlands, Italy (in these areas Jews had previous contacts with left-wing, anti-Fascist movements), France (mostly under assumed names), and Slovakia (revolt of 1944) was patriotic and subconsciously Jewish.

In particular, in the Maquis the Jews were welcome as French patriots, as enemies of the Nazis, and as victims of the Nazi occupation regime. The Jewishness of a candidate was a guarantee for his devotion to the cause. He was more reliable than the average Frenchman from a security viewpoint. No wonder that their role in the movement was out of all proportion to the percentage of Jewish population in France. The Eclaireurs Israélites de France was a small but an effective—avowedly Jewish—group of *résistants*. This was not the situation in the East. Whether ghetto fighters or partisans in the woods, they were guided by unequivocally Jewish motives—rescue of national honor, "a few lines in history books." More sober—but again Jew-

74

ish—was the motivation of Palestinian Jewish parachutists.

The following manifestations of resistance will now be treated separately: physical resistance—revolt; group (and individual) flights from ghettos, mostly to join partisan or the *résistants;* flight of Palestine-oriented youth; and flights from extermination camps.

PHYSICAL RESISTANCE—REVOLT. The behavior of the active resistance groups in the conditions sketched above manifested itself in various ways. With the exception of the Netherlands, where physical resistance—an act of sabotage—occurred early (January–February 1941) and was paid for with 400 Jewish lives (the people were seized at random by the Nazis and shipped to Mauthausen via Buchenwald where all but one perished within a few months), there was no organized armed resistance in the early years of the war. Revolts in Eastern Europe started in major ghettos at the beginning of 1943, at the time the majority of the Jewish population had already been destroyed, but —what is more significant—at a time when France did not yet have its own Maquis and Tito's partisans had not yet become a serious factor. The Warsaw ghetto revolt of April 1943 was the first direct confrontation of local forces with the Nazis. From the viewpoint of rescue, this and the following revolts were of little value (except for those few fighters who survived the unequal fight), the price was high, the influence of the uprising on the Nazis (who, in the light of the unexpected Jewish resistance decided to speed up the process of destruction) was considerable but the purpose— to demonstrate and affirm Jewish honor—was achieved. Their heroic saga is well-known.

Flights from the Ghettos, Joining Partisans. The flights from Polish and Soviet ghettos were of practical rescue value in areas where partisan bands were active (woods and marshes), although the partisans were largely hostile to the Jews (Soviet partisans were more hospitable than Polish but not always), as was the local population, which was the main source of food supply for the groups. The conditions for a Jewish partisan movement were most unfavorable; it could receive no help from a Jewish state or a Jewish army; it had no arms, and the few it could acquire were obtained with difficulties and at great sacrifice; no really concerted action between individual ghettos was possible for ghetto inmates or even for Jews not confined in ghettos in view of the isolation of the Jews. A Jewish partisan—in a generally hostile environment—had no outside help whatsoever, no supply of food, no mobility. Despite these agonies the Jewish partisans gave a good account of themselves and a far from negligible part of them survived.

Flight of Palestine-Oriented Youth. A particular form of defiant behavior vis-à-vis the Nazi and pro-Nazi authorities was that of He-Ḥalutz and other Zionist youth groups, who had to traverse dangerous routes to reach Palestine, whether they came from the West as, for example, from the Netherlands, or from Eastern countries such as Poland and had to make their way via the Carpathian mountains, Slovakia, Hungary, or Rumania, and the Black Sea.

Flights from the Concentration Camps. Finally, the successful flight of 76 (out of a total of 667 attempted ones) Jewish prisoners from concentration camps to bring the world the news of a people being annihilated should be mentioned. The risks involved in the flights of Jews, who, unlike the fleeing Poles and Russians, did not meet with a friendly reception by the local non-Jewish population, were enormous. That a deaf ear was turned to their message reflects on the kind of world they had to appeal to.

Behavior of Jews in Allied Armies. No analysis of Jewish behavior or the "Jewishness" of certain types of behavior would be complete without a look at the behavior of the Jews in the Allied forces. From all the accounts one conclusion emerges: not only did they do their duty like their fellow citizens, but they often excelled in acts of heroism due to the complete identification of the Jewish soldier with the purposes of the anti-Nazi coalition emotionally strengthened by the conviction that he was fighting for his country and for his people too. This is true for all Allied armies and in particular for the Soviet Army, where the Jews were surpassed in number and grade of decorations only by Russians, Ukrainians, and Tartars. In addition, they were instrumental in the creation of national divisions in the Red Army, e.g., Lithuanian, Latvian, and Czechoslovak, constituting there the majority of the volunteers.

POSTWAR TRIALS. There are known cases of Gestapo agents, informers, and police chiefs in Poland with whom the *résistants* dealt summarily during the occupation. Many more had to answer charges after the war.

In the Netherlands, a Jewish Court of Honor tried members of the Joodse Raad and condemned them on several counts, including acceptance of membership in the council. Neither the Courts of Honor in the DP camps, nor the Israel law and practice considered the membership in Jewish councils or police per se as reprehensible. A propos, in Warsaw, people like Czerniakow considered as deserters members of the prewar council (deeply involved in prewar anti-Nazi activities) who had fled abroad. The Joodse Raad members were further condemned for publishing the *Joodse Weekblad* which had become a mouthpiece for the Germans and for participation in the selection and transportation of the Jews to the East, but not for shipping them knowingly to their death.

In the DP camps, Courts of Honor and Rehabilitation commissions were active for a number of years. They were connected with the central and local organizations of DPs in Germany and Italy. The functions of these two types of institutions were supplementary: while the courts considered alleged misdeeds and judged the defendants, the rehabilitation commissions acting on behalf of individuals who felt themselves unjustifiably maligned, ruled on their requests. In both cases the basic approach of the courts was to find whether the respective persons deserved a place in the postwar Jewish community. Persons found guilty were disqualified from participation in the new Jewish organizations, either permanently or for a number of years. In addition, they were denied DP benefits (material assistance, help in emigration) and, in particular cases, were even excommunicated. The number of trials of council members was minimal (as was their percentage among the survivors); most of the trials were against ghetto policemen and *Kapos* (prisoner supervisors or prisoners-functionaries in camps). Some trials were also conducted in Poland and in some countries of resettlement, including Israel where they were based on the above-mentioned law, and were conducted before state courts.

CONCLUSIONS. Subject to the moral reservation (see pp. 58, 59) the following conclusions emerge:

a) While the participation in the Jewish councils was largely determined by a long tradition of communal responsibility, its members and those of the Jewish police were in the last stages faced with demands never made by the Nazis on other institutions created and used by them as instruments of local control. This general survey has discussed the effect of their participation on the final outcome of the Nazi policy of extermination. As for the behavioral aspect of this complex there remains the question of conscience to be considered in each individual case on its own merits.

b) In two aspects the Jewish behavior of the active elite was undoubtedly superior in spirit and objectives: (1) the conscious and deliberate element of self-sacrifice to save the honor of the Jewish people; (2) the quality of the Jewish share in the war on the side of the Allied powers.

c) The behavior of the Jewish masses in the various stages of the Holocaust is in a general way what could have been expected from any group having to face all-pervading terror by the overwhelming power of a ruthless enemy such as the Nazi machine. In two respects it was, perhaps, above expectations. First, the instinctive will to live (in the ghettos where families were not separated) developed resourcefulness and inventiveness in combating famine and oppression hardly found elsewhere in comparable situations. Second, in spite of continuous terror and the bestiality of the persecutors, depersonalization only rarely reached the lowest level of animalization.

d) The comparative instances cited here have illustrated the fact that the behavior of the Jewish masses was not a result of some inherited or racial traits, but was the product of Nazi terror unprecedented both in its objectives and methods.

3 CONCENTRATION
AND EXTERMINATION CAMPS

Though not originally established specifically for Jews, the concentration and extermination camps, from the first, fulfilled a decisive role in carrying out the Nazi policy of exterminating the Jews. Under the Nazi regime in German (1933–45), a system of camps was set up to isolate and intern persons suspected of opposition to the regime; however, it developed into an unprecedented, vast network for the suppression and extermination of millions of persons of various nationalities designated as enemies or specifically as members of so-called "inferior" population groups in the Nazi-dominated and occupied countries.

Protective Custody of Enemies of the State (1933–39). Legal sanction was given to arbitrary imprisonment by the *Notverordnung des Reichspraesidenten zum Schutz von Volk und Staat* (Feb. 28, 1933), which served as a base for "protective custody" by authorizing the unlimited detention of persons suspected of hostility to the regime. The regulation requiring a written protective-custody warrant *(Schutzhaftbefehl)* was introduced on April 12–16, 1934, in order to placate the judiciary, who still demanded that the legality of each arrest be examined. A clause postulated on Jan. 25, 1938, extended protective custody to persons whose conduct endangered the security of the nation and the state for detention solely in the concentration camps. In an order of Feb. 10, 1936, Heinrich Himmler invested the Gestapo with authority to make arrests and investigate activities hostile to the state within the Reich. He also decreed that the Gestapo's orders were not subject to investigation by courts of law and handed over the administration of the concentration camps to the Gestapo. The protective-custody warrant was presented to the detainees, if at all, only after their arrest. They were first sent to prison and tortured for long periods. The detainee was then forced to sign the warrant that was sent to the concentration camp as his dispatch note.

During the night following the declaration of a state of emergency after the Reichstag fire (Feb. 27, 1933), there was a wave of mass arrests of the Communist opposition. After the *Ermaechtigungsgesetz* ("Enabling Act") of March 23, 1933, the non-Nazi political elite, composed of trade-union members, socialists, and civil party members, was arrested, together with Jewish writers, journalists, and lawyers. In July 1933, the number of protective-custody detainees reached 14,906 in Prussia and 26,789 in the whole Reich. The SA (Storm Troops), the SS, and the police improvised about 50 mass-detention camps. Dachau, Oranienburg, Esterwegen, and Sachsenburg were thus created. The worst camp of all was the Berlin Columbia Haus. The methods of arrest, kidnappings, tortures, bribery, and blackmail of associates created chaos and aroused protest in Germany. As a result of pressure from the judiciary, and upon the advice of the then head of the Gestapo, Rudolf Diels, to Hermann Goering, most of the SA and SS *Wilde KZ* ("Wild concentration camps") were broken up. Oranienburg, Lichtenburg, and Columbia Haus remained, containing no more than 1,000 prisoners each.

The reduction in concentration camps was no indication of any move to abolish them; among the new victims of the terror were those who listened to foreign radio stations, rumormongers, Jehovah's Witnesses (*Bibelforscher*, in 1935), and homosexuals. Under the command of Himmler, who on April 20, 1934, took over direction of the Berlin Gestapo, the SS gained total control of the concentration camps, and the judiciary were prevented from intervening in the Gestapo's domain. Small concentration camps were broken up, and their prisoners transferred to larger camps, such as Dachau (which was enlarged), Sachsenhausen (established in September 1936), and Buchenwald (established in August 1937). When the number of concentration-camp detainees dropped to about 8,000 in late 1937, it was augmented by the dispatch of criminal offenders and persons defined as "asocial." In April 1938 ordinary prisoners under preventive detention were transferred from prisons to concentration camps, which, in addition to their original function, then became *Staatliche Besserungs- und Arbeitslager* ("State Improvement and Labor Camps"). At about the same time, Jews qua Jews (not as Communists, Socialists, etc.) were interned in concentration camps for the first time.

The number of political detainees (Marxists, anti-Nazis, and Jews) rose after the annexations of Austria—in March and April 1938—and Sudetenland from Czechoslovakia —in October and November 1938. Overcrowding in the camps grew worse, especially after the arrest throughout the Reich of about 35,000 Jews after the *Kristallnacht* of 1938. The total number of detainees rose that year from 24,000 to 60,000. In 1939 the internment of individual Jews for the slightest violation of the *Schikanengesetzgebung*— irksome special legislation—began. Jews convicted for *Rassenschande* (violation of race purity) were often put into internment camps after having served their sentence. But the specific nature of Jewish internment prior to World War II was the probability of the internee being released if he could prove that he had a chance to leave Germany, and in 1939 the release of Jews possessing emigration papers, who paid exorbitant ransoms, resulted in a marked drop in the number of Jewish internees. With the outbreak of war, the total number of detainees rose to 25,000 (including those in the women's camp of Ravensbrueck, set up in May 1939 in place of Lichtenburg).

World War II. Changes were wrought in the concentration camp system by World War II. There was an increase in the number of prisoners, extension of the network of concentration camps in and outside Germany, and an alteration in the camps' function. The security function (i.e., protective custody) was subordinated to the economic exploitation

Auschwitz. Courtesy Yad Vashem Archives, Jerusalem.

of detainees and mass murder. Under the renewed security pretext, ten times as many political prisoners were arrested in the Reich as had been arrested in the years 1935–36. In the occupied countries, thousands of "opponents" were detained in local concentration camps while special groups were "transferred" in vast numbers to concentration camps within the Reich. From the outbreak of war until March 1942, the number of detainees rose from 25,000 to 100,000 and in 1944 the number reached 1,000,000; only between 5 and 10% of them were German nationals.

Late in 1939 the concentration camp organization in Germany was authorized to set up about 100 concentration camps of all types, including *Internierungslager* (detention or internment camps) and *Austauschlager* (exchange camps). To these were added Auschwitz (May 1940), Gusen (May 1940), and Gross-Rosen (Aug. 1940). That year, a series of Jewish and non-Jewish labor camps was established, together with transit camps *(Durchgangslager)*, as part of Himmler's "transfer and resettlement" plan. In May 1941 Natzweiler was set up, followed by Niederhagen (May 1940), Majdanek (November 1940), Stutthof (November 1940), and Arbeitsdorf (April 1942). In early 1942 there was further expansion, when the extermination camps were set up in Poland. The rate at which camps were established varied but did not decline. Even as late as 1944 *Sonderlager* ("special camps") were established for Hungarian Jews in Austria on the borders with Czechoslovakia and Hungary.

EXTERMINATION. Concentration camps had been fitted out as execution sites even before the plans for mass extermination were formulated. In addition to the execution of individuals, various groups underwent extermination by the so-called *Sonderbehandlung* ("special treatment"). The Euthanasia Program involved the killing of the mentally and chronically ill in concentration camps by injection. Under this cover, healthy people were also frequently exterminated. The experience gained in this campaign was later applied to exterminate millions. The concentration-camp doctors murdered those unfit for work with intravenous injections of phenol, evipan-natrium, and prussic acid. Victims of epidemics were also murdered by these methods. In the women's camp of Ravensbrueck, pregnant

One of the crematoria.

Jewish women were sent to the gas chambers, whereas abortions were performed on non-Jewesses.

From 1941 crematoria were built in several concentration camps. Because of the large numbers of corpses, they were not all dissected before cremation, but nevertheless the *Selektion* provided the physicians in German universities with "specimens" for study and for collection. The *Sonderkommando* ("special squad") of prisoners who worked in the crematoria were always exterminated and replaced by new squads, in order to prevent the leaking of information. At first the squads were made up of Jews and later of Poles.

Camps of a special type were set up late in 1941 for the sole purpose of the extermination of "undesirable" populations. These were from the first equipped with extermination facilities and differed from concentration and labor camps and from those camps with a combined program of concentration and extermination. Before these extermination camps were set up, the *Einsatzkommando* ("mobile killing units"), which accompanied the German army invading the Soviet Union, effected the mass slaughter of about 1,000,000 of the civilian population near the front line. This system was slow, public, and horrifying, however, even for the SS; improved techniques of extermination were therefore introduced. One of these was gassing by carbon monoxide fumes introduced from exhaust pipes into hermetically sealed trailer trucks. This system, which could deal with 1,000 victims a day, had many disadvantages and was discarded in 1942. A second method was that of gas chambers, disguised as shower room facilities, with shower room notices in various languages. At first the gas used was diesel exhaust fumes, and the victims often waited outside for hours in long queues because the motor had broken down. The change over to the use of Zyklon B, a gas employed to destroy insects, supplied by I. G. Farben was made after Himmler's visit to the extermination camps in the summer of 1942, when the rate at which gas chambers and crematoria were built also increased.

Cylinders of Zyklon B gas.

Those marked for *Selektion* and after it were forced to run to the "showers" to the accompaniment of a band playing music. Between 700–800 men and women, elderly people, and children were crammed into a chamber measuring 25 square meters (225 sq. ft). The cylinders of gas were emptied into the chamber through the showers; the gassing took about four to five minutes, depending on the number of persons in the chamber. Terrible shrieks could be heard from the hermetically sealed chamber when those inside began to suffocate and their lungs burst. When the doors were reopened, the *Sonderkommando* entered to take out the corpses. If anyone was left alive, he was beaten to death. The contorted and entangled bodies were separated with axes and sorted, and after rings and gold teeth were removed and hair was shorn, they were piled in tens for inspection and taken out to be burned. Later, furnaces and cremating pits were constructed. As the rate of extermination increased, heaps of ashes accumulated by the pits, whose smoke was visible from far away. The economic exploitation of the corpses involved the extraction of tons of gold teeth and rings, which were sent to the Reichsbank and credited to the SS account; the hair and bones were employed in industry; the ashes were used as fertilizer; and the clothes were sent to other camps after fumigation.

Two-thirds of the extermination program was carried out from 1943, when the probability of German defeat was realized. The rate of extermination, which was subject to the rate of transports, took its toll on the communications

As each transport arrived, S.S. officials made their "selections."   87

system just when the army was in need of it, and the extermination of manpower undermined the war effort.

"MEDICAL" EXPERIMENTS. Pseudo-medical experiments were carried out in a number of camps. Even before World War II interned Jews had been used for pseudo-biological "race research." Upon Himmler's initiative, unlimited supplies of live men and women were put at the disposal of the SS medical organization for the purpose of "medical" experiments in the camps and outside. Under the program of the biological destruction of the "inferior races," Viktor Brack, who had also been one of the heads of the Euthanasia Program, was charged in 1941 with developing a quick system of sterilizing between 2,000,000 and 3,000,000 Jews who were fit for work. The Brack system, employed in Auschwitz by Horst Schumann, consisted of the irradiation of the reproductive organs of men and women. Another system was also tested in Auschwitz by Karl Clauberg, who, during the gynecological examination of women, injected them with matter which burned out the womb. Gerhard Madaus and Ernst Koch worked on the development of an herbal means of sterilization, using *Caladium seguinum;* gypsies were used as guinea pigs. August Hirt worked on shrinking skulls for his collection at the anatomical institute at Strasbourg, for the purposes of "racial research." The "specimens" were put to death at Natzweiler. Upon orders received from the air force, experiments subjecting humans to conditions of high pressure and freezing were held at Dachau, to investigate the possibilities of the survival of pilots. In the name of "medical research," humans were infected with contagious diseases and epidemics, in order to try out new drugs and poisons. The SS doctors also amputated bones and cut muscles for transplantation purposes; they removed internal organs and introduced cancer into human bodies. Those victims who did not die immediately were left to perish from neglect and agony. Some of them survived, crippled or maimed for life.

THE CAMPS AND THE "FINAL SOLUTION." From

December 1941, Jews had been gassed in trucks at the Chelmno extermination camp at a pace that did not satisfy those responsible for carrying out the solution to the "Jewish Question." After the Wannsee Conference (1942), which was convened to smooth the cooperation toward liquidation of the Jews, the establishment of new extermination camps, mainly on Polish soil, was hastened. The first to use gas chambers was Odilo Globocnik, chief of the SS and Police Force in Lublin, who set up a Jewish labor camp in 1940 in the Lublin district. He later transformed this camp into an extermination camp. Between 1942 and 1943 Jews were gassed in Belzec, Treblinka, and Sobibor. Near Vilna, Riga, Minsk, Kovno, and Lvov, there were smaller extermination camps where Jews were executed by firing squads. The large concentration camps became extermination centers, e.g., Majdanek, and the largest of all, Auschwitz, which at the height of the extermination program accounted for about 20,000 victims per day. Adolf Eichmann gave priority to the extermination

Electrified fence inside the camp.

of Polish Jews and those expelled from the Reich, since in their case the problem of transport was nil and particularly because Hans Frank, governor of the General-Gouvernement, was urging that his area be "cleansed" of Jews, whose number he overestimated at 3,500,000. Thus in early 1942 the evacuation of the Polish ghettos began in an operation deceptively termed *Umsiedlung* ("resettlement"), the evacuees being sent to extermination camps. At the time that the operation ended (October 1943), many Jewish labor camps still remained, but all of them were turned into concentration camps in 1944.

The deportations from the rest of Europe to the extermination camps (including transports from concentration camps) began in March and April 1942 and continued until late 1944. At first, those able to work were brought because the construction of the extermination camps had yet to be completed. Following the rebellion at Treblinka (August 1943) and at Sobibor (October 1943) and the advance of the Soviet army, these two camps were abolished together with the Belzec camp, and the extermination center moved westward to Auschwitz and Stutthof. The gassing of Jews continued until November 1944, when it was halted on Himmler's orders.

PRISON LABOR. In 1938, the SS began to exploit prison labor in its DEST *(Deutsche Erd- und Steinwerke GmbH)* enterprise, in coordination with Albert Speer, the man who was responsible for the Nazi construction program for rebuilding Berlin and Nuremberg. This policy determined the sites for new concentration camps—Flossenbuerg, a punishment camp, and Mauthausen establised in mid-1938. The war effort reinforced the function of the camps as a source of manpower for forced labor. Under Oswald Pohl,[14] the concentration camps became centers for the exploitation of the inmates. According to German calculations, the fee for 11 hours (by day or night) of prisoner labor was 6 RM (= $1). The fees from prisoner labor, totaling hundreds of millions of marks, were one of the SS's principal sources

[14] Head of the SS Economic Administration

of income. The SS incurred inconsequential expenses for the prisoner's upkeep, amounting to no more than 0.70 RM daily for food and depreciation in clothing. Taking into account the average life span of a slave laborer (about 9 months) and the plunder of the corpse for further profit, the total income to the SS for each prisoner averaged 1,631 RM. This excluded industrial exploitation of corpses and property confiscated before internment.

Private suppliers of military equipment, such as I. G. Farben, Krupp, Thyssen, Flick, Siemens, and many others used the concentration camps because of the cheap labor and maximum exploitation afforded, so that prisoners constituted 40% of the industries' labor force. Working conditions in private enterprises, worse than those in the concentration camps themselves, were the direct cause of a high death rate. In the Bunawerke (artificial rubber factory) belonging to I. G. Farben at Monowitz near Auschwitz, the manpower turnover was 300% per year. The employers were not authorized to mete out punishment, but with the aid of the *Kapos* they instituted so brutal a system of punishments that the SS sometimes intervened on the prisoners' behalf. Approximately 250,000 concentration camp prisoners were employed in private industry, while about 170,000 were utilized by the Reich Ministry of Munitions and War Production. The death rate in the concentration camps (60% in 1942 and 80% thereafter) appeared excessive even to the Inspection Authority, who, for fear of a depletion of a manpower reserve, were ordered to absorb new prisoners and lower the death rate.

The desire to exploit the prisoners was in direct opposition to the extermination program of "inferior" population groups, and mainly the extermination program against the Jews (the "Final Solution"). This opposition resulted in a continual battle between the employers, the SS-Wirtschafts- und Verwaltungshauptamt ("Economic and Administrative Main Office," WVHA) and the Reichs-sicherheitshauptamt, RSHA, who were responsible for the extermination policy. The scenes of these conflicts were 91 those concentration camps in which mass extermination facilities had been installed, such as Auschwitz, where SS officers and SS doctors sorted out the transports, sending the weak (including children) to their deaths and the able-bodied to work. The latter became camp prisoners and were registered accordingly. They were kept alive for as long as they could work. Reality had created a sort of compromise; the conditions of employment of prisoners helped to kill them and served merely as an extension of life until they completely collapsed and were sent as refuse to the crematories. The concentration camps thus became large-scale extermination centers.

Structure and Administration. On July 7, 1934, Himmler appointed Theodor Eicke inspector of concentration camps and *Fuehrer* of the SS *Wachverbaende* ("guards"). A fanatic, brutal Nazi and efficient organizer, Eicke determined the uniform pattern of the concentration camps, fixed their locations, and headed their inspection authority until his transfer to the front in November 1939. The economic administration, including the financing and equipping of the SS Death Head Unit, members of which served as guards, was handled by Pohl. As a result of conflicts between the Gestapo and SS, a division of tasks was made: the Gestapo made arrests and the SS actually ran the camps. This, however, did not prevent the struggle between the various authorities and the resulting tangle of bureaucracy, which kept the prisoners from knowing which office decided their fate. The different types of concentration camps were classified into three categories in accordance with the severity of their detention conditions. In practice the various camps resembled one another in their inhumanity. Dachau served as the model camp, where guards and commandants were trained. Eicke created a combination of concentration camp and labor camp by exploiting the prisoners for profit and to finance the camps themselves.

The gate of the camp was a one-story construction in the center of which stood a tower with a clock and a searchlight. The gate usually bore a motto, such as "*Arbeit macht frei"* ("Labor makes free"). The parade ground *(Appellplatz)* stretched from the gate to the wooden huts where the prisoners were housed. The structure of the command was fixed in 1936 and included (a) the *Kommandantur,* comprising the *Kommandant,* who held authority over the heads of divisions; (b) the Political Department, an autonomous authority in the Gestapo, responsible for the file cards of the prisoners and, from 1943, in command of executions (it confirmed the lists of Jews chosen through *Selektion* ("selection") for death in the gas chambers); (c) the *Schutzhaftlager* ("protective custody" camp), under command of the *Schutzhaftlagerfuehrer,* whose *Blockfuehrer* were responsible for order and discipline in the prisoners' quarters (there were also *Arbeitsdienstfuehrer,* responsible for the division of labor, and the *Kommandofuehrer,* who led the labor detachments); (d) the administration, which dealt with administration, internal affairs, and economy (Concentration camps that absorbed transports of Jews had a special staff to classify their goods and send them on to the *Hauptversorgungslager* in Auschwitz.); (e) *Lagerarzt,* the SS physician.

Guard duties were carried out mostly by the SS Dead Head Units. In 1944, 1,000,000 prisoners were kept by 45,000 guards, of whom 35,000 were SS men and 10,000 were army or navy men or non-German auxiliaries. The guards were allowed the unstinted use of weapons against escapees or rebels, and if a prisoner escaped the guard was tried, while guards who killed escapees were rewarded.

The prisoners were classified as follows: political prisoners, including smugglers and deserters (after the outbreak of war these included all non-Germans); members of "inferior races," Jews and gypsies, and criminals; asocials, such as tramps, drunkards, and those guilty of negligence at work. Homosexuals constituted a special group. Each group wore a distinctive badge, a number, and a triangle colored according to the different categories. The Jews wore an additional yellow triangle, inverted under the first, thus forming a Star of David. At a later stage, in some concentration camps the prisoner's number was tattooed on his arm.

The prisoners' administration, whose structure resembled that of the concentration camp command, cooperated with the SS, and this structure resulted in dual supervision of the prisoners. Sadists and disturbed persons in an administrative post could brutalize their fellows. The prisoners' administration was headed by a *Lageraeltester* ("camp elder"), appointed by the camp commandant. Each block of prisoners' dwellings had a *Blockaeltester,* assisted by *Stubendienste* ("room orderlies"), who were responsible for maintaining order and for the distribution of food. The work detachments were headed by *Kapos,* work supervisors responsible to the SS *Kommandofuehrer* and assisted by a *Vorarbeiter* ("foreman"). These posts were generally given to criminal offenders, who often exceeded the SS in their brutality, either from sadism or from fear of the SS. The *Kapos* spied on their fellow prisoners and ingratiated themselves with their masters, but their hopes of survival through oppression of their fellow men failed, as they too usually fell victim to the machinations of the SS. In hard labor detachments a prisoner could escape the punishments meted out by the *Kapos* and remain alive only by bribing them. The *Kapos* created a regime of corruption and blackmail, which gave them a life of comfort and ease as long as they held their posts.

The prisoners, who reached the camps in a state of hunger and exhaustion, were forced to hand over the remainder of their personal property and in return received a set of clothing, which included a navy-and-white-striped shirt, a spoon, a bowl, and a cup. They were allotted space in the tiers of wooden bunks in huts containing three or four times the number of persons for which the structures were originally intended. The prisoners' daily life resembled the outside world only in the names given to everyday objects. Horrific realities were often hidden under accepted words as "food," "work," "medicine," and "neutral" words such as *Sonderbehandlung* ("special treatment," i.e.,

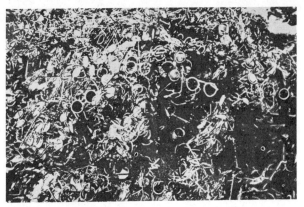

A storeroom of eyeglasses.   A storeroom of shoes.

95

execution) *Selektion* (the selection of those to be sent to their death), or *Desinfektion* (i.e., gassing). The prisoners' diet bordered on starvation and deteriorated further during the war years. The terrible hunger did more than anything else to destroy the human image and even reduced some to cannibalism. The extremely poor conditions of health and hygiene and the lack of water also aided the spread of disease and epidemics, especially typhus and spotted fever. The camp doctor and his prisoner assistant often caused or hastened death through neglect, mistreatment, or lethal injections.

End of the Camps. As the Russians advanced from the east and the British and Americans from the west, Himmler ordered the emergency evacuation of prisoners from camps in the occupied territories. No means of transportation was available for the evacuation, and in early 1945 most of the prisoners were dragged by the thousands in long death marches lasting several days in cold and rain and without equipment or food. The German prisoners were given weapons to help the SS. Exhaustion, starvation, thirst, and the killing of escapees and the weak accounted for hundreds of thousands of victims. The local populations, who had been incited against the prisoners, attacked them and refused sanctuary to those who escaped. At the reception camps, masses of the new arrivals died of starvation and overcrowding, which hastened the spread of epidemics such as typhus and spotted fever. The evacuation operation cost the lives of about 250,000 prisoners, many of them Jews.

The concentration and extermination camps constituted a terrifying example of the "new order" which the Nazis were preparing for the whole world, using terror and the impersonal murder of millions of anonymous victims to turn "ideology" into reality. The murder itself was the end process of the destruction of the victims' identity and their ethical personalities. The splitting of groups into individuals, and individuals into atoms reduced most of the prisoners into mere shadows of men; some became hungry animals fighting for their existence at the expense of their neighbor's lives; others became *"muselmann,"* who had lost the will to live. Nevertheless, there were prisoners, many of them Jews, who had the energy and the ability to organize revolts (as at Treblinka and Sobibor) and try to escape, individually or in groups (e.g., from Auschwitz), but only a small percentage succeeded. When the Reich crumbled there was no one to give the order to exterminate. The SS fled, dragging the remnants of the prisoners with them westward for extermination, in the hopes of destroying all remains of their crime. Only 500,000 concentration camp prisoners and those destined for extermination remained alive, most of them physically crippled and mentally broken. These surviving remnants, together with many documents which authorized the reign of terror, bore witness to the horrors of the phenomenon. Exact data are lacking, but the many accounts and documents confirm the estimate of 4,000,000 Jews put to death in extermination camps, a further 2,000,000 Jews having died in other ways.

Major concentration, forced labor, transit, and extermination camps in Europe, World War II.

Gassing. The idea of systematic and organized extinction of inoffensive human beings, Jews and non-Jews, emanated from the conception which abolished the basic belief in the sanctity of human life and substituted the postulated predominance of the Aryan race whose superior value and whose purity had to be secured. As Hitler said in *Mein Kampf:* "A corrective measure in favor of the better quality must intervene." (Eng. transl. (1939), 248.)

Racial-biological "eugenics" were at first not applied to the Jews but to the elements in the German people itself. The "Law for the Prevention of Progeny with Hereditary Disease" was proclaimed already on July 14, 1933. The problem was further dealt with at the Nazi Party convention on Sept. 1, 1933, where the director of the "Racial-Policy Office" called compassion for people suffering from hereditary disease "false humanity" and a "sin against the Creator's own laws of life."

The implementation of the "Euthanasia Program" was prepared as from July 1939, together with the war. It was a top secret program carried through and supervised by the staff of Hitler's private chancellery. The action included the concentration of the mental patients chosen for the "merciful death" and their transportation from there to the nearest euthanasia station, short "medical" investigation of each patient, mainly in order to decide on the most plausible fictitious "cause of death" and then gassing of 20–30 people at one time in hermetically shut chambers disguised as shower rooms, cremation in the crematorium-annex after gold teeth had been broken off and some of the brains secured for "medical research."

Between January 1940 and August 1941, 70,273 German people were killed in five euthanasia institutions by this *Sonderbehandlung* (special treatment). The carbon monoxide gas was provided compressed in steel containers and released through pipes into the gas chamber. People were dead after 6–7 minutes. The first experiment was done by Kriminal-Kommissar Christian Wirth; later a specially trained chemist, Dr. Kallmeyer, became responsible for the whole gassing process. In August 1941 Hitler called the program officially off following the evolving unrest in the population, legal complications, and mounting protests, especially by the Churches. In fact, the institutions continued to function until 1944 but death was administered partly by gas, partly by injections, and partly by gradual starvation. Also put to death were the chronically ill, gypsies, foreign forced laborers, Russian prisoners of war, children from mixed marriages, and others "unworthy of life."

When in October 1941 the mass-shooting of Jews by the *Einsatzgruppen* (mobile units) became problematic, the three experts of the killing operation came together and decided on the use of gas: Erhard Wetzel, director of the Racial-Policy Office of the Nazi Party and the consultant on Jewish affairs of the Reich Minister for the Occupied Eastern Territories Alfred Rosenberg; Victor Brack, deputy director of the Chancellery of the Fuehrer, the man mainly responsible for the implementation of the euthanasia program; and Adolf Eichmann (Source: NO-997). Since the euthanasia program had just been officially discontinued it must have seemed reasonable to use the experience for the new project. The two technical experts, Christian Wirth and Dr. Kallmeyer, were sent to the East to make the necessary installations. Physicians who had conducted the euthanasia program were also transferred. In the meantime gas had been employed in the fight against partisans in Yugoslavia. Here vans were used into which the exhaust fumes of their diesel engines were channeled. This method was now applied to the first killing center at Chelmno. Then Globocnik seized the idea and used it for the installation at Belzec and Treblinka. Gerstein met Wirth there as the chief operator. Wirth now used the exhaust fumes the way the carbon monoxide gas had been handled in the euthanasia operation installing the whole process with the shower-room camouflage and securing gold teeth and other valuables. Hoess [15] brought the system to perfection in Auschwitz. He went back to the easier use of chemical gas but chose hydrogen cyanide, the so-called Zyklon B crystals, instead of the carbon monoxide, apparently because it could easily be provided in great quantities. He also developed the crematorium scheme which had been in use in the euthanasia installations. Following the semantics of the previous stages the working teams were now called *Sonderkommando*. Zyklon B was also used in minor scale in Majdanek and in the concentration camp Gross-Rosen which was used for the extermination of concentration camp inmates in Germany. The gas chambers in Dachau and Theresienstadt were never put into action.

[15] Nazi commandant of Auschwitz extermination camp

4 ADOLF HITLER

Hitler's extreme anti-Semitism is probably of multiple origin. In *Mein Kampf* (1925–27; Eng. tr. by R. Manheim, 1943), Hitler denies having heard of a Jewish problem in his home or at the school he attended in Linz; but his childhood friend, Kubizek, affirmed that Hitler's father was a follower of the anti-Semitic politician Georg von Schoenerer and that Hitler himself displayed anti-Semitic feelings in school. Various witnesses relate that the

young Hitler read the *Linzer Fliegende Blaetter,* which was notoriously anti-Semitic in content. The anti-Semitism of Hitler's father would appear to be an even more likely source, considering that as a customs official he belonged to the petite bourgeoisie, among whom anti-Semitism was extremely widespread during this period in Austria (as in Germany and other European countries). During 1908–13, when Hitler lived in Vienna, his anti-Semitism seems to have acquired the extreme and distinctly morbid characteristics by which it was later marked.

The rapid rise of Hitler's brand of anti-Semitism in the Viennese period would seem due to political influences, reading, and personal experiences that combined to take hold over a preexisting pathological character. Hitler's own testimony reveals the particular influence of two anti-Semitic politicians over him in this period: von Schoenerer, and the Christian-Socialist leader, the burgomaster of Vienna, Karl Lueger. However, certain witnesses attributed to the reading of *Ostara,* a periodical edited by Joerg Lans von Liebenfels and devoted entirely to the most extreme racial anti-Semitism, a decisive influence on Adolf Hitler. Hitler probably read numerous other anti-Semitic publications in this period. He admitted becoming a confirmed anti-Semite when he "discovered" the Jews' role in the white slave trade, their influence on the Viennese press (which he believed to be anti-patriotic), and their function in the "revolutionary" social democracy. All his observations from then on further reinforced his hatred of the Jews and proved to him their widespread destructive influence. Hitler left Vienna in 1913 to establish himself in Munich. It is unknown to what extent his experiences during World War I influenced his anti-Semitism, but the political situation in the Reich, and in Bavaria in particular, at the end of 1918 and beginning of 1919 further confirmed his hatred of Jews. In fact a considerable number of Jews were at the head of revolutionary movements that threatened to introduce bolshevism in Germany; they played the same role at the head of the revolutionary movements in other countries. In

Munich, where Hitler was stationed from the end of 1918, a large number of heads of the ephemeral Soviet Republic of Bavaria were Jews. Hitler declared that he then felt called upon by Providence to devote his life to the struggle against the Jews. In 1919 he joined a small nationalist, anti-Semitic political circle, the Deutsche Arbeiterpartei (German Workers' Party), and in 1920 he set himself up as the *Fuehrer* of the party, which in the meantime had become the National-Sozialistische Deutsche Arbeiterpartei (NSDAP). The struggle against the Jews would become a central and immutable point of the party's ideology.

Hitler's Myth of the Jews. At the commencement of his political activity in Munich, Hitler became closely allied with the anti-Semitic publicist Dietrich Eckart. Shortly after Eckart's death an incomplete book, *Der Bolschevismus von Moses bis Lenin; Zwiegespraech zwischen Adolf Hitler und mir,* appeared under his name containing Hitler's essential theses on the Jewish problem. Hitler developed the same ideas in *Mein Kampf,* and in a text uncovered in 1961 in manuscript form referred to as *Hitlers Zweites Buch (Hitler's Secret Book,* tr. by S. Attanasio, 1962) as well as in numerous speeches delivered in the period of his struggle for power. All the elements of the myth of the Jew conceived by Hitler were previously used by the German and Austrian anti-Semites at the end of the 19th century, as well as in different forms in works such as the *Protocols of the Elders of Zion* (the German edition of which appeared in 1920). According to this myth, the Jews are an inveterately evil race whose ultimate aim is to destroy the superior "aryan" race and dominate the world. To attain their goal the Jews incessantly work to grasp dominating positions in political life by exerting their powerful economic influence, stirring up wars, and instigating revolutionary movements, of which Marxism is the clearest example. They do not hesitate to undertake a subversive or corrupt enterprise and devote themselves to corrupting the Aryan race by polluting Aryan blood. Hitler, far more than his anti-Semite predecessors, insisted on the danger of "sexual contamination" by Jews and identified the Jew with microbial infection. He believed that the Jews were the "propagators of infections," that they "spread the plague," and possessed nothing on their arrival in Germany "except for infectious diseases." "To hope to come to terms with these ferments of decomposition of peoples" he declared, "is the same as hoping that the human body could, over a period of time, assimilate the germs of the plague." The measures Hitler took in his struggle against the Jews resemble in fact the compulsive rites of identification and purification that can be observed in the mentally ill who believe themselves constantly threatened with contamination. However, Hitler's anti-Semitism stands out more than any other in the systematization and inflexibility of its implementation, leading him to conceive and effect the extermination of Jewry.

The Prelude to the "Final Solution." From 1933 on, Hitler's anti-Semitism is expressed by Germany's National-al Socialist policy. Hitler decided on a systematic "purification" of the Reich by increasingly excluding Jews from German society. The Nuremberg Laws (1935) created the "legal" definition of the Jew and the clear distinction between German and Jew. The "Law for the Protection of German Blood and Honor" forbade any union, whether in the framework of marriage or otherwise, between the two categories defined. All the subsequent anti-Jewish decrees in the Third Reich emanate from the definitions set by the Nuremberg Laws.

During the prewar period, it was possible for Hitler's anti-Semitic measures, over and above their manifestly pathological nature, to serve political ends. Thus, by designating the Jews as the source of all Germany's evils, Hitler blamed the Jews for all the regime's weaknesses by identifying with them all the elements hostile to National Socialism. Making the Jew the symbol of absolute evil, he further encouraged the discrediting of the Jews in the eyes of millions of German anti-Semites. He obligated all Germans to take a stand on the "Jewish question" and in 103 this way strengthened the regime's totalitarian control of the people.

The few difficulties that his extreme anti-Semitism caused the regime on the outside could not counterbalance all the benefits reaped by it internally. But also abroad, as in Poland, the Balkans, and certain circles in Western Europe, German anti-Semitic policy found many supporters. When the war broke out, the completely irrational character of Hitler's anti-Semitism reasserted itself. With the first campaigns in Russia, it appears that he saw the struggle (aside from political and strategic calculations) as an apocalyptic one between the forces of Good represented by National Socialist Germany and the forces of Evil guided by the Jews. Hitler's decision to exterminate all the Jews of Europe should be viewed in this context.

Adolf Hitler and the Extermination of European Jewry. It is not known when Hitler conceived the exact plan for the physical extermination of the Jews. In *Mein Kampf* he wrote that between 12,000 and 15,000 Jews should have been gassed in World War I. On January 30, 1939, he "prophesied" that a new world war would lead to the extermination of the Jewish race in Europe. Thus, the thought of exterminating the Jews was familiar to him. The occupation of Poland put several million Jews at his mercy, and the state of war dispensed with the necessity to reckon with reactions abroad, equally providing for a time the opportunity to act without the knowledge of the bulk of the civilian population in Germany. Heydrich's order, given on September 21, 1939, concerning the territorial concentration of Polish Jewry and mentioning an unclarified "final aim," perhaps already implied a project of physical destruction of the Jews. It would appear that no such project was yet envisaged, since various documents indicate that in the summer of 1940 Hitler approved the evacuation of Jews from the occupied countries to Madagascar. But the Madagascar Plan was quickly abandoned, and at the beginning of 1941, when the Russian campaign was in preparation, the extermination of European Jewry was decided on. It seems that the directive was given orally in March 1941, when Hitler ordered the execution of political commissars captured in the Russian campaign and defined the autonomous role to be played by the *Reichsfuehrer-SS* Heinrich Himmler in the occupied Russian territories.

Hitler followed and controlled every phase of extermination, sometimes even in individual cases. According to Himmler's letter of September 18, 1941 to the *Gauleiter* of Wartheleand, Arthur Greiser, "the Fuehrer desires that the old Reich *(Altreich)* and the Protectorate (Bohemia-Moravia) be rid as quickly as possible of their Jews by an action from west to east." In the autumn of 1942, Hitler personally gave the order to deport Jews employed until that time in armament industries. On June 19, 1943, he repeated his order: "Despite the upset that might result, the evacuation of the Jews must be carried out in the most radical manner."

To his intimate circle, Hitler frequently described the action against the Jews in this period as "one of the greatest revolutions accomplished in the world." According to Hitler, the Germans' struggle was of the same nature as that carried on in the previous century by Pasteur and Koch. He stated that "in exterminating this plague, we are rendering to humanity a service which our soldiers cannot imagine." He hinted at the extermination of the Jews in his discussions with the heads of Germany's satellite states. Thus, in April 1943, he explained to Horthy, regent of Hungary, that "the Jews must be treated like tubercular bacilli, which could contaminate a healthy body." Moreover, in his public speeches, Hitler explicitly referred numerous times to the extermination then in progress: "People always laughed at my prophecies," he declared on November 8, 1942, in reference to his above-mentioned speech of January 30, 1939. "Among those who laughed then," he added, "are innumerable persons who no longer laugh today, and those who are still laughing, will probably soon stop." On February 24, 1943, he was even more explicit: "This struggle," he declared, "will not end with the annihilation 105 of Aryan mankind, but with the extermination of the Jewish people in Europe." Between five to six million Jews were actually exterminated in the framework of Hitler's "Final Solution."

From the autumn of 1944, Himmler made several attempts secretly to stop the extermination of the Jews, while Hitler never rescinded the orders issued for exterminations in 1941 and reacted with the greatest violence to news that reached him concerning attempts to save certain groups of Jews. Until death, the incessant struggle against the Jews seemed to Hitler the supreme task incumbent on the German people. In his political testament, written in his bunker under the ruins of Berlin, he exhorted the German people: "Above all, I bind the leadership of the nation and its subordinates to the painful observance of the racial laws and to merciless resistance against the world-poisoner of all nations, international Jewry."

5 PARTISANS

Jewish partisans were among those who took part in the resistance movement and guerrilla war in Europe against Nazi Germany during World War II. The first nuclei of partisans were composed of individuals or groups that were forced to flee from the Nazis and their collaborators; soldiers who were thrown into areas that were occupied by the enemy; and prisoners of war who escaped from camps. Their natural bases were the forests and swamps of eastern Poland, Lithuania, Belorussia, and the Ukraine, the mountainous areas of the Alps, Yugoslavia, Slovakia, and Greece. While the partisan movement as a whole became a substantial force in the military and political battles of World War II the motivations, organizational forms, and development of the Jewish partisan movement was basically different. Unlike the non-Jews in occupied areas, the Jews were condemned by the Nazis to total extermination. As a result of this situation, two unique aspects of the movement stand out: Jews joined the partisan struggle as a path of revenge on the murderous enemy; they also wished to combine partisan fighting with attempts to save themselves and other Jews.

Jews participated in the partisan movement throughout occupied Europe—from Briansk in the east of the U.S.S.R. to France, Italy, Yugoslavia, and Greece. It is impossible to arrive at exact numbers of Jews in partisan units, but it is possible to conjecture that tens of thousands of Jews fought in the partisan struggle as a whole. The number of Jews who actually fought, however, was only a tiny proportion of the European Jews who wished to participate in and had access to the partisans, but were prevented from doing so for a number of reasons. One should distinguish between subjective obstacles to their participation, which resulted from the nature of the condition of Jewish life in Eastern Europe, and obstructions that resulted from their objective situation and attitude of the non-Jewish environment.

The Jews were a classically urban element. Existence in dense forest, in the wilds of nature, was alien and frightening to them. In addition, the traditionally strong family ties that held them together also held them back from leaving their homes. The youth, who were the prime candidates for escape into the forests, were sometimes the only source of support of the family under conditions of a bitter struggle for physical survival and uncertainty about the future. Moreover, the consolidation of Jews or other groups in the forests was conditional upon a priori factors. A central condition for the establishment of any partisan force was contacts with the inhabitants of the surrounding area. The partisans were in need of safe places of refuge in the event of emergency, loyal sources of intelligence, and the supply of food, horses, etc. All these things could be obtained from villagers who lived near the partisan camps. The villagers would provide the necessary services either out of fear or because they believed that cooperation would be to their benefit in the future. However, the Polish, Lithuanian, Belorussian, and Ukrainian countryside was hostile toward the Jews. The villagers, with the exception of those few who remained loyal to Jews under the most difficult conditions, not only refused to aid the Jews in establishing themselves in the forests, but often turned escaped Jews over to the Germans or murdered Jews who managed to reach the forests and looted their property.

The chances of being accepted into a partisan unit were conditional upon physical strength, military experience, and the possession of arms. The sources of arms were those left by retreating armies and passed into the hands of the movements through the underground or they were private

property. Such arms were not given to Jews, who were thus

forced to acquire weapons from the enemy by illegal purchase, robbery, or acquisition in battle. By these means, it was possible to acquire only the most minimal store of weapons.

The partisan movement itself was not free of anti-Semitism. The extreme right-wing factions of the Polish underground viewed the Jews as "bandits" prowling around the forests. They took arms away from the Jews and even murdered many of them. The leftist groups took a less hostile stand toward the Jews. In Lithuania, Belorussia, and the Ukraine, anti-Semitism was somewhat restrained after permanent contact had been established between the partisan areas and the Soviet high command; but the Soviet command did not approve of the existence of separate Jewish partisan units and obligated the Jews to integrate into the multinational partisan frameworks.

The very act of leaving the ghetto for the forests was bound up with many obstacles and difficulties. The Jewish population in central Poland was far from the areas of dense forest. The attempts by the Jewish Fighting Organization in Warsaw, Częstochowa, and Zagłębie to establish contact with Polish underground organizations and smuggle groups of Jewish fighters into the forests most often ended in failure; the fighters were captured or murdered before they could reach their destination or early in their stay in the forest. In the large ghettos in Warsaw, Vilna, and Bialystok, a sharp dispute took place among the members of the Jewish Fighting Organization over which path to choose: resistance inside the ghetto or escape to the forests and carrying on the struggle within the ranks of the partisan movement. In Warsaw it was finally decided to concentrate all forces for resistance within the ghetto; in Vilna and Bialystok a two-pronged method was arrived at, i.e., after the uprising in the ghetto the surviving fighters turned to the forests.

The most important obstacle that prevented the mass escape of the Jews to the forests was a chronological factor. The expansion and strengthening of the partisan movement

Partisan fighters forced out of their bunkers

Captured partisans awaiting their fate

The burning ghetto

Photographs taken by General Stroop during his subjugation of the ghetto, April–May 1943. Courtesy Yad Vashem Archives, Jerusalem.

Es gibt keinen jüdischen Wohnbezirk – in Warschau mehr!

From Stroop's report to Hitler: "There is no Jewish quarter in Warsaw any more!"

began only during 1943. By then most of the Jews in Europe had already been deported to or exterminated in the Nazi death camps. Although the Jews had in many cases been the first who paved the way in the forests, these pioneer partisans had only limited chances of absorbing large groups of people and maintaining their existence for a longer period.

In Western Europe the obstacles were of a different nature, for there the Germans succeeded in deceiving the Jews by well thought-out devices. The resistance movement mostly took the form of an urban underground, which was not to the benefit of the Jews.

However, despite all the obstacles and stumbling blocks, tens of thousands of Jews reached the ranks of the partisan movement. Many Jews fought as individuals (sometimes hiding their Jewish identity) in mixed partisan units, while others belonged to separate Jewish units or groups of Jews united in larger partisan frameworks. Many Jewish partisans rose to commanding ranks and were among the parachutists sent by the Soviet High Command to organize and command partisan camps in large areas. A number received medals for their leadership, and their names and feats of heroism became legendary.

Among the Jewish groups were some that had organized earlier in the Jewish Fighters' Organizations in the ghettos (the *Fareinkte Partizaner Organizatsie* [F.P.O.] in Vilna, the organizations in Bialystok, the remnants of the Jewish Fighting Organization after the Warsaw ghetto uprising). They were equipped and trained during their stay in the ghetto, and their later struggle in the forests was but a logical continuation of the path they had chosen. There were also groups and camps of Jews, mostly from small townlets, who had escaped in whole families or individually during the deportations or from a camp. Together with the youth who were engaged in actual fighting were Jewish family camps in the forests. These camps absorbed women and children, the aged and sick, and a small number of fighters who protected them and provided for their indispensable needs. Most of the time these family camps existed under the aegis of fighting Jewish units or large partisan battalions whose commanders demonstrated a humane attitude and sensitivity toward Jews.

Many Jewish fighters tried to combine their war against the enemy with extending aid to the surviving Jews who were still hiding in the ghettos and in taking revenge against people who were known to have murdered Jews or turned them over to the Nazis. In many cases, Jewish units that established themselves in the forests became the focal point 113 for uniting prisoners of war and members of other nationalities and constituted the beginning of a powerful partisan center. There were about 15,000–20,000 Jewish partisans in the area under the control of the Soviet command. A large partisan concentration existed in the forests of Rudnik around Vilna. Groups of fighters from the F.P.O. reached this area in September 1943 and formed the fighting Jewish Brigade, which consisted of four battalions, under the command of Abba Kovner. Earlier, a group of fighters under the command of Josef Glazman, had left the ghetto and merged with an existing Jewish group to form the fighting group Nekamah ("Revenge") in the forests of Narocz. The commander of the unit, which was later disbanded, was B. Boyarski. Members of the Kovno ghetto underground also reached the forests of Rudnik. These partisans crystallized into a Jewish bloc in the "Lithuanian Brigade," which consisted mostly of Jews.

During 1943 those in the forests surrounding Bialystok were practically all Jews. A group of young women active in the underground in the city helped to supply them. Surrounding Slonim in the forests of Lipiczansk were a number of Jewish units and Jewish family camps. The most famous of these units was that under the command of Jehezkiel Atlas, who cooperated with the Pobeda ("Victory") unit. Atlas' company gained much experience in battle. In the forests of Lipiczansk, an area of western Belorussia, the group under the command of Hirsch Kaplinski, which numbered more than 100 people—most of them from the town of Zheteil (Dyatlovo)—was also active. In central Belorussia, in the forest area of Naliboki, was a large camp of Jewish fighters. In the autumn of 1943 its membership reached more than 1,000, some of whom were fighters and the rest members of the family camp. This camp functioned under the leadership of the Bielski brothers and was composed of simple people from the tiny townlets in the area. Later on, the camp was divided into a fighting company named after Ordzhonikidze and a family camp named after Kalinin.

In the swamplands of Polesie, Jews were active in general units and separate Jewish ones. The Jewish units were formed by the escapees from the townlets. In a small townlet in the center of Polesie, Lachva, about 600 Jews revolted and fled in the direction of the forests. Only about 120 of the youth succeeded in reaching the forests with one rifle and one revolver among them. In Volhynia, Jews were among the first fighters in the forests. The emissary Konishtschook who arrived from the Minsk area to organize partisan action in Volhynia, united Jewish youth from the neigboring townlet. The most daring military offensives were those of the unit commanded by M. Gildenman, which was a branch of Suborov's forces.

An important chapter in the annals of the partisan movement was contributed by the Jews of Minsk. The Jews who organized the underground in the Minsk ghetto were among the key organizers of the partisan movement in Soviet territory. There were also a number of Jews in many Soviet brigades. Many Jews were in positions of command and the fighters in the General Kowpak camp. Jewish survivors from the Skalat ghetto joined this camp during its march over the Carpathians and established the 7th Jewish Brigade of the Kowpak camp.

Within the boundaries of the Polish General Government, Jewish units were active in cooperation with the leftist People's Army. Most of these units were active in the Lublin and Kielce areas. Many individual Jews filtered through to the units of the military underground of the Polish government-in-exile in London, but this organization did not encourage the escape of Jews into the forests, and its extremists even pursued and murdered Jews.

About 2,000 Jews fought in the ranks of Tito's partisan movement, and a number of Jewish groups even existed independently for a period of time. Moshe Piade was one of Tito's first and closest collaborators. In September 1943 a group containing a few hundred fighters and a substantial number of nurses formed the Jewish "Rab Battalion" within the Italian concentration camp on the Adriatic 115 island by that name. They joined the partisans as a well-organized unit, but later dispersed and fought in various units. According to official figures, 250 Jews fought with general partisan units in Bulgaria. In Italy as well Jews were scattered among the Italian fighters. Eugenio Caló from Pisa was the founder of a partisan unit in the Val di Piana, and among its members was Emmanuele Artom. Another Italian Jew, Giulio Bolaffi, from Turin, founded and commanded the "4th Alpine Battalion" that was active in the area of the Vale d'Suza in Piedmont.

Jews were among the founders of the partisan movement in Slovakia. The beginnings of this movement were in 1942, but the partisan struggle in Slovakia became a full-scale war in the summer of 1944 with the national Slovak rebellion. Members of many national groups fought in this uprising, including about 2,500 Jews. Two Jewish labor camps—Sered and Novaky—were in the area liberated by the partisans and organized Jewish units, and the inmates of these camps joined the rebellion. At the height of the uprising, four parachutists from Palestine reached Slovakia; two of them remained in Slovakia and the other two passed into Hungary. The two who remained in Slovakia fell into the hands of the Nazis on their way to the last center of the rebels in Banska in Bystrica; both were shot in November 1944. After the rebellion was suppressed in October 1944, the partisans retreated to the mountains. There were 2,000 Jews (out of a total of 15,000) in the ranks of the Slovak partisan movement after the uprising.

The participation of Jews in the French Resistance was substantial—constituting only about 1% of the total population of France, at one stage Jews composed about 15–20% of the Resistance. It is necessary to distinguish between Jews who joined general organizations and units of the Resistance and those who formed independent Jewish units.

In contrast to the situation in several East European countries, Judaism was not an obstacle to accepting candidates into the ranks of the French Resistance.

Nonetheless, most Jewish fighters preferred to suppress the fact of their origin, either for security reasons or because they felt their identity as Frenchmen more important than their identity as Jews.

The role of Jews both in the ranks of the Resistance and in positions of leadership and command was outstanding. Among the six men who founded the organization called Libération were three Jews. At the time of the liberation of France, there were at least three Jews among the 16 members of the National Committee, the highest institution of the underground. Jean-Pierre Lévy was the founder of the Franc Tireurs. The commander of the Franc Tireurs et Partisans Français (F.T.P.) in the Paris region in 1942–43 was "Colonel Gilles" (the underground name of Joseph Epstein of Warsaw). The leader of the F.T.P. in Toulouse, who fell during the uprising toward the end of the liberation, was "Captain Philippe" (Ze'ev Gottesmann). The French underground hero, Jacques Bingen, whose name was commemorated on a stamp bearing his image, left France in 1940, joined De Gaulle's forces, and returned in 1943 as head of the Free French delegation in the northern region.

Among the independent Jewish groups, a distinction should be drawn between Jewish Communists from Eastern Europe and Jewish groups that united on the basis of national and religious motives. The groups of Jewish Communists, opposing the party line of alliance with Hitler (until June 22, 1941), formed a number of commando units that operated in Paris in 1942–43. These groups of the F.T.P., and, in the south, groups of the Jewish Organization for Resistance and Mutual Aid engaged in daring and efficient actions, such as the execution of Nazi officers and collaborators, mining railroad tracks, and raids on enemy arms' depots.

A distinct nationalist Jewish character was the sign of a movement whose nucleus was composed of members of the Jewish Scouts, Zionist youth movements, and members of the He-Ḥalutz[16] from Holland who had reached France.

[16] Zionist Socialist pioneering movement

The movement of Jewish Scouts at first engaged in welfare activities and "passive resistance." It aided in the evacuation of Jewish children from Paris to provincial towns, forging documents, and smuggling Jews over borders, but eventually it did not content itself with these activities and together with the Armée Juive, established the Organization Juive de Combat (O.J.C.).

Robert Gamzon established the Jewish Maquis. This unit entered into action with the landing of the Allies on French shores, attacking the retreating German forces and capturing an armed German train. Other groups of the O.J.C., whose headquarters were in Toulouse, were established in Paris, Lyons, Grenoble, Marseilles, Chombron, Nice, and other cities. The O.J.C. testified to carrying out 1,925 actions, including 750 instances of sabotaging trains, destroying 32 factories that worked for the enemy, and blowing up 25 bridges. It also executed 152 militiamen, traitors, and secret agents (including General Phillipo, a German spy). In 175 actions against the Germans, it killed 1,085 of the enemy's men. In addition, as a result of the organization's activities, the German army lost seven planes (blown up on the ground), 286 trucks, and more than 2,000,000 liters of gasoline. Groups of the O.J.C. also participated in the battles for the liberation of Marseilles and Grenoble.

6 RESCUE

In October 1933 the League of Nations established the "High Commission for Refugees (Jewish and Others) Coming from Germany" which was headed by James G. McDonald. When the commission failed to achieve any significant result, McDonald resigned in protest on Dec. 27, 1935.

Another attempt at international action was made by U.S. President Roosevelt who called an intergovernmental conference on refugee problems held at Evian-les-Bains on the French shore of Lake Geneva in July 1938. Roosevelt's emissary, Myron Taylor, was in the chair during the weeklong deliberations of the representatives of 32 European and Overseas countries. Representatives of 39 refugee organizations were present, among them 20 Jewish bodies who presented memoranda, describing the Jewish plight under Nazi rule and suggesting solutions. The memorandum of the Jewish Agency for Palestine pointed out the country's prospects for agricultural and industrial development and expressed "the earnest hope . . . that this Conference . . . will pay special attention to the great possibilities offered by Palestine for the solution of the Jewish problem." Still, under British pressure, nothing of this kind was contemplated by the conference. At this time, as also during the following crucial years, Roosevelt's behavior was ambivalent. Neither he himself nor his even more hostile advisers from the State Department had any intention to amend the United States' harsh immigration law which had been introduced after World War I. Under pressure from Jewish and non-Jewish circles (outstanding among the latter was Dorothy Thompson), it was tried **119** "to find ways and means of making a gesture that would neither inherently hurt us nor provoke retaliation [on the part of Germany] that would hurt us." So the Secretary of State Cordell Hull and his deputy Sumner Welles "decided that it would be inadvisable for the Department to attempt merely to resist the pressure, and that it would be far preferable to get out in front and attempt to guide the pressure, primarily with a view toward forestalling attempts to have the immigration laws liberalized." Still, at the same time Roosevelt also gave the order to handle the immigration regulations more liberally, and this trend was intensified after the conference, so that at least the legal quota was fulfilled. While in the period July 1, 1932–July 1, 1937 something less than 20,000 Jews entered the United States, there were more than 63, 000 Jewish immigrants in the two fiscal years of 1938 and 1939.

From the outset it had been stated by the conference's organizers "that no country would be expected or asked to receive a greater number of immigrants than is permitted by the existing legislation." It is therefore not very astonishing that the practical result of the conference was very meager. Australia agreed to receive 15,000 immigrants in three years, but actually only 9,000 entered in the period from 1933 to 1943. Most of the Latin American countries as well as the Europeans were only ready to add insignificant numbers. The one exception was the Dominican Republic, which declared itself ready to settle up to 100,000 agricultural immigrants. A special Settlement Association—sponsored by the American Jewish Joint Distribution Committee (JDC)—acquired land in the northern part of the island. In spite of the large sums which JDC contributed, the project could not be carried through, and by 1942 less than 500 settlers had reached the land. Still, the 5,000 visas which had been issued helped to rescue their recipients even though they did not reach the Dominican Republic.

The main outcome of the conference was the establishment of a permanent Intergovernmental Committee on

Refugees, headed by the American lawyer George Rublee. The committee's seat was London, where it worked in close connection with the representative of the British government, Lord Winterton. It succeeded in reaching an international agreement on travel permits for those refugees who were not in possession of a passport. Rublee's main attempt was the implementation of the so-called Schacht-plan, called after its promotor, the German minister of economics and president of the Reichsbank, Hjalmar Schacht. The plan was conceived when the urge for emigration grew strong among the Jews in Germany after *Kristallnacht* (Nov. 9–10, 1938). It was based on the facilitation of the transfer of Jewish assets from Germany by linking it to the promotion of German export. To this end the foreign Jewish bodies were supposed to raise a loan in foreign currency, based on the estimate of Jewish property in Germany, the greater part of which was supposed to remain in Germany. The scheme was supposed to finance the emigration of 150,000 able-bodied Jews and 250,000 dependents in the course of three years. The plan did not materialize. With Hitler streamlining his administration in early 1939 toward the planned war, Schacht was dismissed from his cabinet post. In addition the Jewish leaders were reluctant to take an obligation upon themselves that could be interpreted by the Nazi propaganda as visible proof for the alleged international financial Jewish conspiracy. In addition, they, as well as officials in the respective governments, objected to making confiscated Jewish property the basis for increasing German export. Rublee, who had meant to help the Jews, resigned, and the League of Nations' High Commissioner for Refugees, Sir Herbert Emerson, took over. The negotiations dragged along until they were terminated by the outbreak of the war.

In May 1939 Britain's White Paper on Palestine restricted Jewish immigration to Palestine to 75,000 over the next five years. "Illegal" immigration to Palestine began in earnest in 1938, but only 15,000 had arrived by the time the war broke out. After the outbreak of 121 war (September 1939) and until early 1941, about 12,000 additional Jews were rescued by "illegal" entry. An abortive attempt was made in 1942 to bring 769 Jewish refugees to Palestine on the freighter *Struma*, but Britain refused to admit them to Palestine and Turkey and sent the boat into the Black Sea where it sank on February 24, with the loss of all on board.

While closing the gates of Palestine Britain provided or also pretended to provide other opportunities. From the summer of 1938 to the outbreak of the war and even after, various plans for Jewish settlement in remote places of the world were launched. These included the British suggestion to settle Jews in Guiana. They did not propose the coastal region, which comprises 4% of the area but holds 90% of the population, nor the open region adjacent to it. The land considered was situated in the forest and swamp region, in spite of the fact that an international commission in 1935 had found it unsuitable for the settlement of 20,000 Assyrians who suffered from persecution in Iraq. Nevertheless the Intergovernmental Commission sent an international investigating committee to explore the area. Still, in May 1939, just before the White Paper on Palestine was published, the British Prime Minister Neville Chamberlain announced that Jewish settlement in British Guiana had good prospects to create a new community enjoying autonomy and representation. If the British really thought that this "new Balfour Declaration," as it was sometimes called, would compensate the Jews for the projected loss of the "National Home" in Palestine, they were naive. In any case they dropped the project, quickly explaining that the natives objected and that the region was needed for the settlement of the inhabitants of the West Indies. A representative of the JDC had taken part in the inquiry commission. More was done by Britain for the reception of Jewish refugees in England itself, especially after *Kristallnacht*, when thousands of Jews had been thrown into concentration camps. About 8,000 of them could be freed by leaving Germany immediately for

England, where they were initially accommodated in reception camps. This was one of the successful actions of the English Jews' Council for German Jewry, which had been organized in May 1933 under the name of Central British Fund for German Jewry. The Council bore most of the costs for the support of the refugees, who numbered, at the time of the outbreak of the war, about 60,000, the largest number received in any single European country.

With the outbreak of the war, control of aliens everywhere was heavily tightened, and there was strong opposition to admitting more refugees for fear of a fifth column. In France and Great Britain all foreigners from German-ruled territory were interned. In England only part of them were released reluctantly under public pressure when identified as anti-Nazi refugees. The United States was swamped by a sort of public hysteria of anti-alien feelings and the State Department's Breckinridge Long, who headed the Special War Problems Division, made it his personal task to curtail immigration. According to his own words he "won all the battles and the war in the immigration fight." That meant that even the conceded immigration quota was only 75% filled. Roosevelt's own behavior was again ambivalent. He took measures to ensure "more effective control over aliens," and Congress even outdid him in this endeavor by passing bills putting more and more obstacles before the prospective immigrant. On the other side, under pressure of Jewish organizations and some public voices, the president also tried to act independently from his administration and intervened to admit hundreds of specially recommended people. It is to the credit of the Jewish efforts that during 1939–41, the American Jewish Joint Distribution Committee and HICEM managed to rescue over 30,000 European Jews, most of whom reached the U.S. via Italy, and from June 1940, via Portugal and Spain. Between the summer of 1940 and early 1941 some 4,400 Polish Jews escaped from Lithuania to Japan and the U.S., and a few hundred went to Palestine via Odessa. A number of

Polish Jews left the U.S.S.R. in 1942 with the Polish army of General Anders, including 850 children, mostly orphans, who reached Palestine in 1943. After the entry of the U.S. into the war, escape to the West was limited to those who were already in neutral countries. Immigration to Palestine in late 1942 and 1943 was limited to 350 Jews from Europe. News regarding the Holocaust became generally known only in late 1942, and on December 17 the Allies issued a declaration condemning the mass murders; however, no concrete attempts to rescue Jews were made by the Allies until early in 1944.

The situation of the refugees had of course worsened considerably with the United States' entry into the war. Every humanitarian consideration was dropped, and the slogan "rescue through victory" became the statement of official policy. This policy did not take into account that few Jews would remain to be rescued after victory. An Anglo-American conference on the refugee question was held in Bermuda in April 1943 while the remnants of the Warsaw ghetto were fighting their desperate fight. As in Evian it was the main intention of the conference, which had been sponsored by the British, to counteract "the deep sentiments on the part of the Jews." But even this was not achieved, because it soon became obvious that nothing had been decided apart from the reconstitution of the Intergovernmental Committee. The delegates avoided referring to the Jews as the Nazis' special victims, concerning themselves mainly with general post-war refugee problems.

An offer that had been made by Eichmann's deputy in Bratislava, Dieter Wisliceny, to the working group of Jewish leaders there to purchase the rescue of the Jewish remnant in Europe, was transmitted to the U.S. government but the matter was not followed up. In 1943 and 1944 attempts were made both by Jewish organizations and by individuals in Switzerland to send South American passports or nationality papers to individual Jews in Europe. Individuals, mainly in Poland, Holland, and Belgium were also informed that Palestine immigration certificates were waiting for them. A number of South American governments refused to take steps to protect the holders of these mostly false papers, and only in 1944 did this attitude change. Nevertheless, small groups of bearers of these papers were kept by the Nazis in special camps, and some of them survived the war. From Switzerland, and partly also from Lisbon, a number of bodies such as the JDC, the Jewish Agency, the Orthodox Va'ad ha-Ḥazzalah, and others corresponded with and sent parcels to Jews. He-Ḥalutz in Geneva was instrumental in procuring information and contacts necessary for rescue work. The JDC also transferred funds to underground Jewish organizations in Europe with the approval of the United States. Yielding to pressure, President Roosevelt appointed a War Refugee Board (WRB) in January 1944 which financed relatively small-scale rescue schemes and the sending of food parcels and funds for underground rescue operations. Early in 1944 Ira A. Hirschmann, the WRB delegate in Turkey, and the International Red Cross in Bucharest aided in bringing back 48,000 Jews from Transnistria to Rumania. In Istanbul a center for rescue was developed in 1943–44 dealing largely with immigration to Palestine. Jewish Agency emissaries and others smuggled out over 3,000 people via Istanbul before the liberation of Rumania in August. In May 1944 Joel Brand [17] was sent from Hungary to negotiate with the Allies on a German offer to trade Jews for trucks and others wares. Official negotiations were vetoed by the Soviets, but talks began in Switzerland between Saly Mayer, the JDC representative, and an S.S. delegation under Kurt Becher with Himmler's knowledge. As a result of the talks 1,691 persons were brought from Hungary to Switzerland via Bergen-Belsen, and 17,000 others were brought to Vienna under more or less tolerable conditions. In February 1945 an additional 1,200 were brought out of Theresienstadt by the pro-German Swiss statesman, Jean-Marie Musy. In June 1944, the WRB

[17] Member of the Budapest Jewish relief committee during World War II   125

helped obtain the intervention of Sweden, Switzerland, the Holy See, and the International Red Cross which, along with a strong American warning, persuaded the Hungarian government to stop the deportations of Hungarian Jews in July. However, the demands transmitted by Roswell McClelland, the WRB representative in Switzerland, and the Jewish Agency to bomb the Auschwitz murder installations and the railways leading to it were refused, though in fact factories adjacent to the camp were bombed in September. In the autumn and winter of 1944 representatives of neutral governments in Budapest, among them Raoul Wallenberg of Sweden and Charles Lutz of Switzerland, cooperated with Zionist youth groups in preserving the lives of many thousands of Jews who were equipped with genuine or forged "protection" papers.

The Jewish Agency called for sending Jewish Palestinian parachutists to Europe, but its request was rejected, except for 32 men and women who were sent in 1943–44 to the Balkans, Hungary, and Slovakia. The parachutists' missions failed on the whole because they were too few in number and came too late; seven of them were killed by the Nazis. Between 20,000 and 30,000 Jews escaped from France to Spain and Portugal between 1940 and the summer of 1942; from 1942 on over 11,000 more escaped until the summer of 1944. About 11,000 entered Switzerland in 1942–44. The Jewish underground in France, supported by the JDC and other bodies, facilitated these rescue operations. In October 1943, the Danish underground shipped over 7,000 Danish Jews to safety in Sweden. Several hundred Norwegian Jews were also smuggled into Sweden. In late 1944 and early 1945 Norwegian, Danish, and Swedish efforts, coupled with the intervention of Himmler's Finnish masseur Felix Kersten, led to the evacuation first of Scandinavians and the Danish Jews from Nazi camps and then of thousands of women from Ravensbrueck camp, including 1,500 Jewish women. This latest success was made possible by the personal encounter between Himmler

126 and the representative of the World Jewish Congress'

branch in Sweden, Norbert Masur, who flew in April 1945, together with Kersten, to Berlin and faced the strategist of the mass murder.

On the whole, rescue operations achieved little until 1944, because the Allies were indifferent to the problem. Inactivity was explained by the argument that only a German defeat would rescue the oppressed and that any diversion of energies from the war effort for rescue activities might diminish the successful conclusion of the war.

In the U.S.S.R. The absolute number of Jewish survivors in the Soviet Union was greater than that in any other European country. For several years after the war rumors spread, largely by Communist propaganda sources, claiming that the Soviet government had made a special effort to rescue Jews from the Nazis or to evacuate them from the advancing German armies. These claims have been shown to be unfounded. Those Jews who escaped Nazi extermination on Soviet soil (including, until June 1941, Soviet-occupied territories in eastern Poland, the Baltic states, north Bukovina, and Bessarabia), did so either by fleeing eastward from the advancing Germans, often encountering Soviet guards who drove them back, or, after June 1941, by being evacuated into the Soviet interior as Soviet administrative personnel or as skilled workers. The Soviet authorities never accorded special help to Jews in order that they might escape Nazi persecutions.

On Sept. 17, 1939, when the Red Army entered eastern Poland, there were in that region hundreds of thousands of Jews who had fled from the German occupation in western Poland, and tens of thousands more were streaming in. The Soviets maintained an open border until the end of October, when the two-way traffic of Jews and non-Jews between the two occupied sectors came to a halt. When this movement ended, and only Nazi-persecuted Jews continued to pour into the Soviet side, the Soviets closed their border and forced the new refugees to return to the German sector, many of whom perished between the lines. The Jewish refugees from western Poland numbered about 300,000–

400,000. They were ordered to choose between accepting Soviet citizenship or returning to their previous homes in the western sector, though the Soviets knew (but the refugees did not) that the Germans categorically refused to accept them. The refugees were not offered the alternative of a temporary asylum in Soviet territory. Since the Soviet authorities extended practically no assistance to the homeless refugees, most, particularly those who left close relatives behind, felt compelled to register for return to their previous places of residence in German-occupied territory. For this "demonstration of disloyalty" the Soviets punished the refugees by deporting them to the Soviet interior. Most of the refugees were arrested in June 1940; families were sent to small, isolated villages in the far north of the Soviet Union, and single people were sent to prisons and concentration camps. An event which typifies the Soviet policy of ignoring the Nazi attitude toward the Jews occurred on Dec. 31, 1939, at Brest Litovsk. In this city the Soviets handed over to the Gestapo several hundred Communist activists from Germany and Austria, both Jews and non-Jews, who had found refuge in the U.S.S.R. before World War II.

On the eve of the German-Soviet war (June 1941), thousands of Jews, together with non-Jewish "bourgeois" and "unreliable" elements from eastern Poland and the annexed Baltic states and Rumanian provinces, were deported to and imprisoned in the Soviet far north and far east. As a result many of the deportees escaped the later Nazi occupation of their places of origin (1941–45).

After the outbreak of the German-Soviet war, the Soviet government, under an agreement with the Polish government-in-exile, ordered (on Aug. 12, 1941) the release of Polish citizens from camps and places of exile. Of those released, the Jews were generally barred from joining the newly formed Polish army, which later left the U.S.S.R. Many Jews thereby suffered from lack of food and housing, in spite of the welfare services extended by the Polish embassy and its representatives in the Soviet provinces.

When Stalin announced the "scorched earth" policy and the evacuation of administrative personnel, vital industries, and their equipment and workers, Jews were more interested in speedy evacuation than non-Jews. Jews did exploit the few possibilities available for evacuation; the authorities, however, did not grant any priority to Jews. Soviet Jews, i.e., residents and citizens of the U.S.S.R. in its pre-September 1939 boundaries, could, on their own initiative, try to escape eastward. However, along the pre-1939 border in Belorussia, the Ukraine, and the Baltic states patrols were set up to prevent refugees who were not officially evacuated from escaping into the Soviet interior. This blockade affected mainly Jews, because very few non-Jews in these areas were eager to flee from the advancing Germans. The number of Jews moving eastward, either on their own initiative or within the framework of the evacuation of administrative personnel and vital industries, increased as the German advance slowed down. It is estimated that of the Jewish residents of the German-occupied areas of the Russian Soviet Federated Socialist Republic (RSFSR) about 50% managed to flee from the Germans. Among the Soviet anti-German underground in the cities and the partisans in the forests there were serious cases of discrimination and enmity toward Jews, sometimes resulting in executions on the basis of unfounded accusations. Some Jewish partisans, nevertheless, succeeded in establishing "family camps" for noncombatant Jews—the elderly, women, and children—who were smuggled out of the ghettos, particularly in Minsk and other places in Belorussia. There were exceptions to the rule of enmity and indifference shown toward the Jews in several German-occupied cities, e.g., Minsk, where Belorussian women organized the hiding of several scores of Jewish children, and Vilna, where individual Jews, particularly children, were saved by clergymen, intellectuals, and domestics working in Jewish homes. Some Soviet partisan commanders helped Jews escape; and in some cases partisan units, particularly those with a considerable number of Jewish fighters, attacked German-occupied townlets in order to rescue their Jewish inhabitants. In the western Ukraine (former East Galicia), there was an outstanding example of organized hiding of some 150 Jewish children, initiated by Andreas Szeptycki, the Ukrainian head of the Uniate Church in German-occupied Lvov. Szeptycki openly preached and protested against the extermination of the Jews and, after being approached by two rabbis, instructed the Uniate monks and nuns to hide Jewish children in their monasteries.

Jews who fled from the German-occupied territories annexed to the Soviet Union in 1939–40 were accorded by the Soviets the same harsh treatment given to western Ukrainians and other residents of those areas who had collaborated with the Nazis. Many of these Jews were sent to the "labor army," which was in fact a system of slave labor camps whose inmates included criminals. Jewish refugees from the Baltic areas and other countries were conscripted into the Lithuanian and Latvian divisions, the Czechoslovak brigade, and the Polish army established in the U.S.S.R. in 1943 after Moscow severed relations with the Polish government-in-exile in London. In many of these military units, Jews constituted the majority of the soldiers and suffered a high proportion of casualties. Jewish refugees from Germany and Austria were treated as "enemy citizens" and sent to forced labor camps. Because they had served on work teams of the pro-German Hungarian army, although forcibly conscripted, Hungarian Jews captured in 1943 on Soviet territory were treated as "enemy prisoners" together with the routed Hungarian units. The Soviets accorded the Jews the same treatment as the Hungarian soldiers even though the Jews were not considered military personnel, wore civilian clothes, the yellow armband, and had been maltreated by their Nazi and Hungarian commandants.

The unreliability of Soviet censuses in regard to the number of Jews in the U.S.S.R. makes it difficult to calculate the number of Jews who managed to escape Nazi extermination on Soviet soil. Figures of the number of Jews saved, published in the West from Soviet sources (e.g., 1,500,000 mentioned by Itzik Fefer[18] in the New York Yiddish *Morgen-Frayheyt,* Oct. 21, 1946), were probably greatly exaggerated. In spite of the official Soviet attitude, a considerable number of Jews nevertheless survived the Holocaust because they found themselves on Soviet soil and somehow succeeded in evading the Germans.

[18] Soviet Yiddish poet and representative of the Jewish anti-Fascist Committee

7 THE CHRISTIAN CHURCHES

The Catholic Church. In response to Hitler's anti-Semitic policies, Pius XI, like the German episcopate, seems to have limited his concern to Catholic non-Aryans. The encyclical *Mit brennender Sorge* (= "with burning anxiety") of March 1937 rejected the myths of "race" and "blood" as contrary to revealed Christian truth, but neither mentioned nor criticized anti-Semitism per se. Nor was anti-Semitism mentioned in the statement of the Roman Congregation of Seminaries and Universities (issued on April 13, 1938) attacking eight theses taken from the Nazi doctrine as erroneous. On Sept. 7, 1938, during a reception for Catholic pilgrims from Belgium, Pius XI is said to have condemned the participation of Catholics in anti-Semitic movements and to have added that Christians, the spiritual descendants of the patriarch Abraham, were "spiritually Semites." This statement, however, was omitted by all the Italian papers, including *L'Osservatore Romano*, from their accounts of the pope's address.

The elevation of Cardinal Pacelli to the papacy as Pius XII in the spring of 1939 brought to the throne of St. Peter a Germanophile who, in contrast to his predecessor, was unemotional, dispassionate, and a master of the language of diplomatic ambiguity. The Vatican received detailed information about the murder of Jews in the concentration camps from 1942 on, but Pius XII restricted all his public utterances to carefully phrased expressions of sympathy for the victims of injustice and to calls for a more humane conduct of hostilities. In his Christmas message of 1942, the pope spoke of his concern for the hundreds of thousands who, without personal guilt and merely on account of their nationality or descent, were doomed to death. Again, addressing the College of Cardinals in June 1943, the pontiff mentioned his twofold duty to be impartial and to point out moral errors. He had given special attention, he recalled, to the plight of those who were still being harassed because of their nationality or descent and who, without personal guilt, were subjected to measures that spelled destruction.

The pope's policy of neutrality encountered its crucial test when the Nazis began rounding up the 8,000 Jews of Rome in the autumn of 1943. Prior to the arrests, the Nazis told the Jewish community that unless it raised 50 kilograms of gold within 36 hours, 300 hostages would be taken. When it seemed that the Jews themselves could raise only part of this ransom, a representative of the community asked for and received an offer of a loan from the Vatican treasury. The pope approved of this offer of help, which, as it later transpired, did not have to be invoked.

During the German authorities' hunt for the Jews of Rome, Pius XII, contrary to German fears, remained silent. On Oct. 18, 1943, over 1,000 Roman Jews—more than two-thirds of them women and children—were transported to the death camp, Auschwitz. About 7,000 Roman Jews were able to elude their hunters by going into hiding. More than 4,000, with the knowledge and approval of the pope, found refuge in the numerous monasteries and houses of religious orders in Rome, and a few dozen were sheltered in the Vatican itself. The rest were hidden by their Italian neighbors, among whom the anti-Jewish policy of the Fascists had never been popular. Pius' failure to publicly protest against Nazi atrocities, especially against the murder of the Jews, drew criticism. In July 1942, Harold H. Tittmann, the assistant to Roosevelt's personal representative at the Holy See, Myron C. Taylor, pointed out to the Vatican that its silence was endangering its moral prestige. In January 1943, Wladislaw Raczkiewicz, president of the Polish government-in-exile, appealed to the pope to issue an unequivocal denunciation of Nazi violence in order to strengthen the willingness of the Poles to resist the Germans and help the Jews. Bishop Preysing of Berlin, a man of courage and compassion, urged the pope on at least two occasions to issue a public appeal on behalf of the Jews. A similar request with regard to the Hungarian Catholics was directed to Pope Pius in September 1944 by Isaac Herzog, the chief rabbi of Palestine.

After the end of World War II, Pius XII was again criticized for his silence. It has been argued—among others, by the German playwright Rolf Hochhuth—that the pope could have saved numerous lives, if indeed he could not have halted the machinery of destruction altogether, had he chosen to take a public stand and confront the Germans with the threat of an interdict or with the excommunication of Hitler, Goebbels, and other leading Nazis belonging to the Catholic faith. As an example of the effectiveness of public protest, it is possible to cite the resolute reaction of the German episcopate to the euthanasia program. In Slovakia, Hungary, and Rumania, the forceful intervention of papal nuncios, who threatened the pro-Nazi governments with public condemnation by the pope, was also able, albeit temporarily, to halt the deportations. At the very least, it has been suggested, a public denunciation of the mass murders by Pius XII broadcast widely over the Vatican radio, would have revealed to Jews and Christians alike what deportation to the east actually meant. Many of the deportees might thus have been warned and given an impetus to escape, many more Christians might have helped and sheltered Jews, and many more lives might have been saved.

No way of proving or disproving these arguments exists, of course. Whether a papal decree of excommunication against Hitler would have dissuaded Hitler from carrying out his plan to destroy the Jews is doubtful, and revocation of the Concordat by the Holy See would have bothered Hitler still less. However, a flaming protest against the massacre of the Jews, coupled with an imposition of the interdict upon all of Germany, or the excommunication of all Catholics in any way involved with the apparatus of the "Final Solution" would have been a more formidable and effective weapon. This was precisely the kind of action that the pope would not take, however, without risking the allegiance of the German Catholics. Given the indifference of the German population to the fate of the Jews and the highly ambivalent attitude of the German Church toward Nazi anti-Semitism, a forceful stand by the pope on the Jewish question might well have led to a large-scale desertion from the Church. The pope had other, perhaps still stronger, reasons for remaining silent. In a world war that pitted Catholics against Catholics, the Holy See, as Mr. Tittmann was told by highly placed officials of the Curia, did not want to jeopardize its neutrality by condemning German atrocities, and the pope was unwilling to risk later charges of having been partial and contributing to a German defeat. Moreover, the Vatican did not wish to undermine Germany's struggle against Russia. Late in the summer of 1943, the papal secretary of state declared that the fate of Europe was dependent upon a German victory on the Eastern front. The Apostolic delegation in Washington warned the American Department of State in a note dated August 20, 1943, that Communism was making steady headway in Italy and Germany, and Europe was in grave peril of finding itself overrun by Communism immediately upon the cessation of hostilities. Father Robert Leiber, one of Pius XII's secretaries, later recalled (in *Stimmen der Zeit*, March 1961) that the pope had always looked upon Russian Bolshevism as more dangerous than German National Socialism. Hitler, therefore, had to be treated with some forbearance.

The reluctance of Pius XII to be drawn into a public protest against the "Final Solution" stands in contrast to the often energetic rescue activities of several of the papal nuncios in Slovakia, Hungary, Rumania, and Turkey. Monsignor Roncalli, the nuncio in Istanbul, who later became Pope John XXIII, in particular helped save many thousands of lives. The extent to which these men acted upon instructions from Rome is not clear, but the motives for the Vatican's solicitude seem to have been mixed. It appears that from late 1942 on, the Vatican was well aware that an ultimate Allied victory was inevitable. Considerations of expediency began to reinforce whatever moral revulsion the pope may have felt at the massacre of the Jews, and Pius began to drop hints to the bishops of Germany and Hungary that it was in the interest of their people, as well as that of the Church, to go on record against the slaughter of the Jews. For example, he wrote an Austrian churchman on Oct. 15, 1942, that to intercede for those suffering in the conquered territories was not only a Christian duty but ultimately could only be of advantage to the cause of Germany.

The Nazis' assault on European Jewry occurred in a climate of opinion conditioned by centuries of Christian hostility to Jewish religion and people. At the same time, other factors, such as varying patterns of nationalism, had an important bearing on the attitude of the Catholic churches of different European countries toward the Jewish tragedy. Thus it is important to differentiate between the situation in Germany and in the various Nazi-occupied countries of Europe. During the 19th century some elements of German Catholicism contributed toward the emergence of modern anti-Semitism, and in the 1920s many Catholic publicists agreed with the Nazis on the importance of fighting Jewish liberalism and the Jews' alleged destructive influence in German public life. This trend received great impetus after Hitler's accession to power in 1933. Seeking to counter the Nazis' offensive against the Catholic Church, as a rival for the loyalty of the German people, churchmen attempted to gain favor with the Nazi regime and its followers by adopting certain aspects of Nazi ideology. They stressed the elemental values of race and racial purity, and limited their dissent to insisting that this National Socialist goal be achieved without resort to immoral means. The sacred books of the Old Testament, it was argued, were not only beyond the Jewish mentality but in direct conflict with it. Jesus, it was conceded, had been a non-Aryan, but the son of God was fundamentally different from the Jews of his time, who hated and eventually murdered him. They also said that the Jews had had a demoralizing effect on Germany's national character; the press, literature, science, and the arts had to be purged of the "Jewish mentality."

In the face of the Nazis' anti-Semitic legislation the Church retreated, even when the ordinances touched on vital domains of ecclesiastical jurisdiction, such as matrimony. The diocesan chancellories helped the Nazi state to detect people of Jewish descent by supplying data from Church records on the religious background of their parishioners. The bishops facilitated the emigration of non-Aryan Catholics, but little, if any, solicitude was shown for non-Aryans who were not of the Catholic faith. Similarly, when mass deportations of German Jews began in October 1941, the episcopate limited its intervention with the government to pleading for Christian non-Aryans. When the bishops received reports about the mass murder of Jews in the death camps from Catholic officers and civil servants, their public reaction remained limited to vague pronouncements that did not mention the word Jews. An exception was the Berlin prelate Bernhard Lichtenberg, who prayed publicly for the Jews. The joint pastoral letter of the German episcopate of August 1943, for example, spoke of the right to life and liberty, which should not be denied even to "men of foreign races and descent" but such statements could be interpreted as referring to the Slavs. Almost half the population of the greater German Reich (43.1% in 1939) was Catholic and even among the S.S., despite Nazi pressure to leave the Church, almost a quarter belonged to the Catholic faith. While in the past the episcopate had issued orders to deny the sacraments to Catholics who engaged in dueling or agreed to have their bodies cremated, the word that would have forbidden the faithful, on pain of excommunication, to go on participating in the massacre of Jews was never spoken. The bishops had demonstrated their willingness to risk a serious clash with the Nazi regime by protesting the extermination of the insane and retarded in the "euthanasia" program. This intervention had been successful in large measure because it had had the backing of public opinion. In the case of the Jews, however, it was far from clear whether the episcopate could count on the support of the faithful, and this was probably one of the main reasons why a clear public protest against the "Final Solution" was never issued. Only a handful of Jews were hidden by the clergy or helped by individual Catholics in Germany. In Poland, where no official policy on the part of the Catholic Church has been discerned, it would seem that, as in Germany, the initiative to help Jews was taken only by individuals. This situation stands in marked contrast to that prevailing in Nazi-occupied Europe. In Western Europe declarations of solidarity and help for the Jews were almost universally regarded as signs of patriotism and resistance to the Germans. Here some of the highest Church dignitaries condemned the persecution of the Jews. In Holland, where the Church as early as 1934 had prohibited the participation of Catholics in the Dutch Nazi movement, the bishops in 1942 immediately and publicly protested the first deportations of Dutch Jews, and in May 1943, they forbade the collaboration of Catholic policemen in the hunting down of Jews, even at the cost of losing their jobs. In Belgium members of the episcopate actively supported the rescue efforts of their clergy, who hid many hundreds of Jewish children. Several French bishops used their pulpits to denounce the deportations and to condemn the barbarous treatment of the Jews. Throughout Western Europe numerous priests and members of the monastic clergy organized the rescue of Jews, and hid them in monasteries, parish houses, and private homes. French priests issued thousands of false certificates of baptism. Many lay Catholics in France, Holland, Belgium, and Italy acted similarly, thus saving thousands of Jewish lives. The concern of the population of these countries for

Jewish fellow-countrymen was undoubtedly a key factor

behind the bold protests of the French, Dutch, and Belgian bishops.

In Eastern Europe anti-Semitism had deeper roots, and the record of the Catholic churches there is more ambiguous. In Slovakia, a Catholic priest, Dr. Josef Tiso, was president of a pro-Nazi regime; the Church there was more interested in saving souls than lives, although the episcopate did protest the deportations as a violation of human and divine law. Several Hungarian bishops protested to the authorities the deportation and mistreatment of the Jews but at the same time put difficulties in the way of issuing conversion certificates that would have saved many Jews from deportation. Large numbers of Jews, nevertheless, owed their lives to the courageous rescue activities of lesser clerics, monks, and Catholic laymen.

Protestant and Greek Orthodox Churches. Protestant churches and their leaders in Britain, the United States, France, Switzerland, and Sweden protested against the first anti-Semitic measures in Germany, the promulgation of the Nuremberg Laws, and *Kristallnacht* of 1938. In Germany, Hitler's supporters within the Protestant Church complied with anti-Jewish legislation, applying it even within the Church by going so far as to exclude Christians of Jewish origin from membership. Although the "Confessing Church" (Niemoeller's dissident *Bekenntniskirche*) defended the rights of Christians of Jewish origin within the church, it generally neither publicly opposed discrimination against them outside the church, nor condemned the persecution of Jews. An exception to this rule was the memorandum sent by the "Confessing Church" to Hitler (May 1936), which stated that "when, in the framework of the National-Socialist ideology, anti-Semitism is forced on the Christian, obliging him to hate the Jews, he has nonetheless the divine commandment to love his neighbor." A number of ministers of the "Confessing Church" were sent to concentration camps because they did not cooperate with anti-Jewish directives. During the war, the Protestants in Germany maintained their silence, the notable exception 139 being Bishop Wurm of Wuerttemberg, who intervened on behalf of the so-called "privileged non-Aryans," in 1943.

In the occupied countries, however, the situation was different. The Lutheran churches in Norway and Denmark issued a public protest when the deportations from their countries began. The Protestant churches in the Netherlands, together with the Roman Catholic Church, sent several protests, some of which were read from the pulpits. In France, the president of the Protestant Federation, the Rev. Marc Boegner, sent letters to the French chief rabbi, to Admiral Darlan, Marshal Pétain, Pierre Laval, and others. A message was read from the pulpits twice. The persecution of the Orthodox Serbs in Yugoslavia matched in cruelty the persecution of Jews. It has been reported that Orthodox Church leaders stood up for the Jews, but hardly any details are available. In Greece, the archbishop of Athens, Damaskinos, headed a group of prominent citizens who sent a strong protest against the deportations of the Jews to the prime minister of the puppet regime and to the German representative in Athens. The contents of these protests show that they were based mainly on national, rather than on religious, considerations. Damaskinos was personally active in the rescue of individual Jews. The bishop of Salonika, Genadios, also intervened on behalf of Jews. The attitude of nonresistance of the population of Salonika, however, shows that the faithful did not always follow the example of their leaders.

SATELLITE COUNTRIES. The Lutheran Church in Slovakia protested in November 1939 and in May 1942. Rumania has a long record of anti-Semitic activities in which leaders and members of the church frequently participated. However, the metropolitan of the Bukovina region, Tot Simedrea, the metropolitan of Transylvania, Balan, and Patriarch Nicodemus personally and successfully intervened with the Rumanian government on behalf of the Jews after fervent appeals from Chief Rabbi Safran. In Bulgaria, the metropolitan of Sofia, Stephan, and the metropolitan of Plovdiv, Kyril, intervened personally with King Boris using extremely forceful expressions. The "Holy Synod of the Bulgarian Orthodox Church" repeatedly sent strong protests in writing to the government. According to a Jewish spokesman, Joseph Geron, the Orthodox Church played a major role among the "collective factors" that helped in the rescue of the Bulgarian Jews. In Hungary, the bishops of the Reformed and Lutheran churches voted in the upper house for the first and second anti-Jewish laws in 1938 and 1939. They protested when mass deportations began in 1944, but, due to government pressure, a prepared public statement was not read out from the pulpits. In the neutral countries the Church of Sweden strongly protested against the deportation of the Norwegian Jews. In Switzerland, protests of the Protestant churches were a factor leading to the alleviation and ultimate canceling of the government measures against Jewish refugees entering Switzerland "illegally," who were at first sent back to their doom. The churches also rendered material aid to the refugees. In Great Britain, the archbishop of Canterbury, the bishop of Chichester, and other church leaders voiced strong protests, but their demands for practical steps were of no avail. The same is true of the United States, where church leaders issued many protests. The World Council of Churches, then still in process of formation, had offices in New York, London, and Geneva. The general secretary, Willem Visser 't Hooft, and the director of the Department for Refugees, Adolf Freudenberg, sent three letters to the International Red Cross, in which they reported on deportations and mass executions of Jews and pleaded for help. Together with Gerhart Riegner of the World Jewish Congress, Visser 't Hooft sent an aide-mémoire to the governments of the U.S.A. and Great Britain, informed church leaders in these countries about the extermination of Jews, intervened with the Swiss government on behalf of Jewish refugees, and helped send gift parcels to Jews in concentration camps.

The non-Roman Catholic churches in Austria, Belgium, the Protectorate (Bohemia-Moravia), Finland, Italy, Poland, and Russia apparently did not issue any public protest during World War II. Individual Christians rendered practical help, though the importance of this fact should not be overrated: only a small minority of the Protestant and Orthodox Christians in occupied Europe risked their lives on behalf of the persecuted Jews. It is difficult to assess the practical results of interventions and protests by churches and church leaders. In satellite countries, where they could turn to their own governments, the interventions of church leaders were of some avail. In the occupied countries, the protests hardly influenced the German authorities; but, in so far as they were read out from the pulpits, the protests contributed to breaking the silence and complacency that surrounded the extermination of the Jews and stirred the faithful to noncooperation with the Germans and to render individual aid to the Jews.

Part Two
THE AFTERMATH

8 WAR CRIMES TRIALS

Crystallization of the Principles of International Criminal Law. When the first Nazi violations of the laws and customs of war as defined by the Hague and Geneva Conventions were revealed (and in particular as they affected the noncombatant population and prisoners of war), official notes, warnings, and declarations began to be published by the Allies. On Sept. 3, 1939, Czechoslovakia's president-in-exile, Eduard Beneš, sent a letter to the prime minister of Great Britain, Neville Chamberlain, reporting the persecution of his country's civilian population at the hands of the Nazis. In 1940 several statements were published by the governments of Great Britain, Poland, Czechoslovakia, and France on the violations of the laws of war in Poland. Crimes against Jews were likewise mentioned. These governments warned Germany and stressed the responsibility of the Nazi regime for the criminal acts. On Oct. 25, 1941, the president of the United States—then a neutral nation—stated that "the Nazi treatment of civilian population revolts the world," while Winston Churchill declared that "retribution for these crimes must henceforward take its place among the major purposes of the war."

After the German invasion of the Soviet Union and the ensuing crimes against the civilian population and prisoners of war, the Soviets also began to publish statements on the subject. The Soviet foreign minister, V. Molotov, declared in his notes of Nov. 7, 1941, and Jan. 6, 1942, inter alia, that the Soviet government held the leaders of Nazi Germany responsible for the crimes committed by the German army. One of the important steps toward retribution can be seen in the St. James declaration made in London on Jan. 13, 1942, in which the representatives of the governments-in-exile of Belgium, Holland, Yugoslavia, Norway, Greece, the Netherlands, Luxembourg, Poland, Czechoslovakia, and of the Free French Committee declared that the punishment through the channels of organized justice of criminal acts perpetrated by the Germans against civilian populations is among the principal war aims of the signatories. Also present at the St. James Conference were representatives of belligerent but non-occupied countries, among them Great Britain and the U.S. The St. James declaration did not specifically mention the crimes against the Jews. This policy of *Totschweigen* ("hushing up the Jewish tragedy") aroused Jewish opinion in the U.S. and Great Britain, and a protest against this policy was lodged on Feb. 18, 1942. Only on Dec. 17, 1942, did the British foreign secretary, Anthony Eden, make a statement in the House of Commons (published simultaneously in London, Moscow, and Washington) on the physical destruction of Jews. Another important step toward this objective was the publication of the Moscow declaration of Nov. 1, 1943, in which the three principal powers, Great Britain, the United States, and the Soviet Union, solemnly committed themselves to the punishment of those responsible for the war crimes. The Moscow declaration distinguishes between criminals whose acts were committed within the boundaries of specific countries and the "major criminals" whose "offenses have no particular geographical location and who will be punished by a joint decision of the governments of the Allies."

The first international body to deal with preparations for punishment of the criminals was the United Nations War Crimes Commission (UNWCC). A proposal for its formation was announced in October 1942 and it was constituted on Oct. 20, 1943. Its objects were to investigate and record the individuals responsible. Participants in the commission were representatives of Australia, the United States, Belgium, Great Britain,

Denmark, India, Holland, Yugoslavia, Greece, Luxembourg, Norway, New Zealand, China, Poland, Czechoslovakia, France, and Canada. The Soviet Union, embroiled in controversy over the composition of its representation, did not join the commission.

Lists of Nazi criminals were drawn up, and it was suggested that governmental and political organizations in their entirety also be included as criminal organizations; membership in these organizations sufficed to brand a man a criminal to be included in the commission's list. The commission's work was carried out through three committees: Committee I: Facts and Evidence; Committee II: Enforcement; Committee III: Legal. In addition there was a Far Eastern and Pacific Commission.

The various Allied activities culminated in the London Agreement of Aug. 8, 1945, which established the International Military Tribunal, and in its charter, which dealt with substantive and procedural rules of the Tribunal. One of the decisive contributions toward the formulation of the revolutionary principles of Nuremberg was made by Hersch Lauterpacht,[19] who defined the three crimes in the charter (crimes against peace, war crimes, and crimes against humanity). In his studies and books he formulated the "Nuremberg principles," which were accepted not only in the London Charter but also in the development of international criminal law in general. The first comprehensive description of violations of international military law was offered by Raphael Lemkin[20] in his book *Axis Rule in Occupied Europe* (1944). It was also Lemkin who coined the term genocide, which was not adopted by the courts but served as the subject of a special international convention. The main theoretical and practical work in the field by world Jewish institutions was done by the Institute of Jewish Affairs of the World Jewish Congress. The political department of the Jewish Agency also collected incriminating material, prepared lists of war criminals, and presented

[19] Professor of international law at Cambridge
[20] Professor of law at Yale

them to the institutions of the Allies dealing with the location and trial of Nazi criminals.

Trials in the Allied Courts and Liberated Countries, 1943–1949. Nazi war crime trials began during World War II itself. The first trial of perpetrators of crimes against civilian populations was conducted in the liberated territories of the Soviet Union. The trial dealt with the abominations committed by the Nazi invaders in the city of Krasnodar. It opened on July 14, 1943, after the liberation of the northern Caucasus, with 11 accused, of whom eight were sentenced to death. The second trial dealing with annihilation of civilian populations and prisoners of war took place in the city of Kharkov, the Ukraine, in December 1943. Three Germans, members of the S.S. and the police, and a Russian collaborator were tried, and all were sentenced to death by hanging. At this trial, for the first time, the world was shown the use of gas for the annihilation of civilian populations.

The specific question of war crimes and crimes against Jews as crimes against humanity within the framework of the general policy of the infamous "Final Solution" was considered only after World War II, first by the International Military Tribunal at Nuremberg (Nov. 20, 1945–Oct. 1, 1946), which tried the heads of the Nazi regime (political, military, and economic leaders) captured by the Allies. The defendants included: Hermann Goering; Hans Frank, governor general of occupied Poland; Ernst Kaltenbrunner, head of the Reich Main Security Office (R.S.H.A.); Joachim von Ribbentrop, Reich minister for foreign affairs; Julius Streicher, gauleiter of Franconia and editor of the *Stuermer,* the infamous anti-Semitic publication; Martin Bormann, chief of the chancery of the Nazi Party (tried *in absentia*). Some of the prominent Nazi criminals and government leaders managed to evade justice and were not brought to trial at Nuremberg: Adolf Hitler, Heinrich Himmler, Joseph Goebbels, and Robert Ley committed suicide; Reinhard Heydrich, charged by Goering with the implementation of the "Final Solution," was assassinated

A session of the International Military Tribunal, Nuremberg, 1945–46. In the dock are: 1) Hermann Goering, 2) Rudolf Hess, 3) Joachim von Ribbentrop, 4) Wilhelm Keitel, 5) Ernst Kaltenbrunner, 6) Alfred Rosenberg, 7) Hans Frank, 8) Wilhelm Frick, 9) Julius Streicher, 10) Walter Funk, 11) Hjalmar Schacht, 12) Karl Doenitz, 13) Erich Raeder, 14) Baldur von Schirach, 15) Fritz Sauckel, 16) Alfred Jodl, 17) Franz von Papen, 18) Arthur Seyss-Inquart, 19) Albert Speer, 20) Constantin von Neurath, 21) Hans Fritzsche. Second from left in front of the dock is defense counsel Robert Servatius, who later defended Adolf Eichmann. Courtesy Yad Vashem Archives, Jerusalem.

in 1942; Heinrich Mueller, one of the heads of the Gestapo, disappeared without leaving a trace.

In accordance with the principles of the London Charter of Aug. 8, 1945, an indictment was lodged together by the four principal prosecutors of the four main powers, and it detailed the accusations against each of the defendants, as well as against six organizations defined as criminal: the Reich cabinet, the Leadership Corps of the Nazi Party, the S.S., the S.A., the Gestapo and S.D., and the General Staff and High Command of the German Armed Forces. In the preparation of the material, as well as during the trial, the four prosecutors had the cooperation of the delegations of the other members of the anti-Nazi alliance and some representatives of Jewish organizations, in particular the World Jewish Congress' Institute of Jewish Affairs headed by Jacob Robinson. The latter assisted in the preparation of the material and in the formulation of the statement concerning the persecution and extermination of the Jews.

The proceedings continued for about a year and were concluded on Oct. 1, 1946, which happened to be the Day of Atonement, with a judgment in which 12 defendants were sentenced to death, three to life imprisonment, four to various prison terms, and three acquitted. The verdicts were carried out by hanging on Oct. 16–17, 1946, except for Goering, who took poison before he could be executed. The charter of the International Tribunal at Nuremberg served as a basis for *ad hoc* laws in countries in which trials of war criminals were conducted (except for West Germany, which did not officially adopt the Nuremberg principles). The International Military Tribunal at Nuremberg and the four-power cooperation did not continue after the judgment, due to differences of opinion between the powers.

The material (proceedings, affidavits, and documents) of the IMT was published in an official edition in 42 volumes in English, French, and German (Eng. title, *Trial of the Major War Criminals*) between 1947 and 1949 ("Blue Series") and constituted an invaluable contribution to the administration of justice to Nazi criminals in various countries, as well as to the study of the Nazi regime and the Holocaust.

The Nuremberg judgment constitutes an important historical turning point, one of the great landmarks in the development of international law and international relations. The IMT went into detail in exposing the whole process of criminal measures against the Jewish people and did not camouflage the Jewish case behind such devices as "victims of racial persecution," "stateless persons," or other euphemisms. In this respect it served as a binding precedent that was followed in other trials almost everywhere. On the other hand, the IMT followed the law of the charter and considered as "crimes against humanity" only such crimes that were somehow connected with "crimes against peace" or "war crimes," in other words with crimes

INTERNATIONAL MILITARY TRIBUNAL

THE UNITED STATES OF AMERICA, THE FRENCH REPUBLIC,
THE UNITED KINGDOM OF GREAT BRITAIN AND NORTHERN
IRELAND, and THE UNION OF SOVIET SOCIALIST REPUBLICS

— *against* —

HERMANN WILHELM GÖRING, RUDOLF HESS, JOACHIM
VON RIBBENTROP, ROBERT LEY, WILHELM KEITEL,
ERNST KALTENBRUNNER, ALFRED ROSENBERG, HANS
FRANK, WILHELM FRICK, JULIUS STREICHER, WALTER
FUNK, HJALMAR SCHACHT, GUSTAV KRUPP VON
BOHLEN UND HALBACH, KARL DÖNITZ, ERICH RAEDER,
BALDUR VON SCHIRACH, FRITZ SAUCKEL, ALFRED
JODL, MARTIN BORMANN, FRANZ VON PAPEN, ARTHUR
SEYSS-INQUART, ALBERT SPEER, CONSTANTIN VON
NEURATH, and HANS FRITZSCHE, Individually and as
Members of Any of the Following Groups or Organizations to
which They Respectively Belonged, Namely: DIE REICHS-
REGIERUNG (REICH CABINET); DAS KORPS DER PO-
LITISCHEN LEITER DER NATIONALSOZIALISTISCHEN
DEUTSCHEN ARBEITERPARTEI (LEADERSHIP CORPS
OF THE NAZI PARTY); DIE SCHUTZSTAFFELN DER
NATIONALSOZIALISTISCHEN DEUTSCHEN ARBEITER-
PARTEI (commonly known as the "SS") and including DER
SICHERHEITSDIENST (commonly known as the "SD"); DIE
GEHEIME STAATSPOLIZEI (SECRET STATE POLICE, com-
monly known as the "GESTAPO"); DIE STURMABTEILUNGEN
DER NSDAP (commonly known as the "SA"); and the
GENERAL STAFF and HIGH COMMAND of the GERMAN
ARMED FORCES, all as defined in Appendix B of the Indictment,

Defendants.

First page of the indictment for the Nuremberg Trials. Courtesy
Yad Vashem Archives, Jerusalem.

committed after the outbreak of the war. Consequently, no attention was paid to such crimes as the April 1, 1933 boycott, the Nuremberg laws, the *Kristallnacht,* etc.

On Dec. 20, 1945, the four Allied governments in occupied Germany enacted the Control Council Law No. 10, which had special significance for the continuation of the Nazi trials and the definition of "crimes against humanity." This law, with minor modifications, eliminated the connection between crimes against humanity and the two remaining crimes (crimes against peace and war crimes), and raised the crime against humanity to a level equal to that of the other two. This extended the chronological validity of the law from the war years alone to the entire Nazi period. The Central Council Law No. 10, whose articles deal mainly with crimes against humanity, enabled each of the Allies, as well as military and civilian tribunals, to hold trials in conquered territories in Germany.

In Allied Courts. Twelve trials (known as Subsequent Nuremberg Proceedings) of special significance were conducted in the American Zone. These were against groups of Nazi criminals who had the chief responsibility for the crimes and were tried by the "Nuremberg Military Tribunals" (composed of U.S. judges) between 1946 and 1949.

1. The Medical Case, Nov. 21, 1946–Aug. 20, 1947.
2. The Milch Case, Dec. 20, 1946–April 17, 1947.
3. The Justice Case, Feb. 17–Dec. 4, 1947.
4. The Pohl Case, March 10–Nov. 3, 1947.
5. The Flick Case, April 19–Dec. 22, 1947.
6. The I. G. Farben Case, Aug. 14, 1947–July 30, 1948.
7. The Hostage Case, July 8, 1947–Feb. 19, 1948.
8. The RUSHA Case, Oct. 10, 1947–March 10, 1948.
9. The *Einsatzgruppen* Case, July 3, 1947–April 10, 1948.
10. The Krupp Case, Sept. 17, 1947–April 10, 1948.
11. The Ministry Case, Nov. 15, 1947–April 14, 1949.
12. The High Command Case, Dec. 30, 1947—Oct. 28, 1948.

During all these trials, acts of cruelty and the annihilation of Jews under the Nazi regime were deliberated. The Jewish question has special significance in the following trials: 4 (Pohl and his accomplices), in which the criminals were tried for committing crimes against the inmates of the concentration and death camps, and especially against Jews; 9, the trial of 24 S.S. and Gestapo men from the *Einsatzgruppen* who headed firing squads that murdered hundreds of thousands of Jews in the conquered Nazi territories in Eastern Europe, and particularly in the Soviet Union; likewise, trial 11 (the Ministry Case), with 21 defendants, molders of Reich policy, who were tried for abetting the preparation of the war and creating the conditions for the implementation of the crimes of the Nazi regime. In the last trial R. Kempner, one of the chief U.S. prosecutors, presented to the Tribunal and the entire world one of the most important Nazi documents from the files of the German Foreign Ministry relating to the annihilation of the Jews, the "Final Solution." It was the record of the Wannsee Conference of Jan. 20, 1942, during which cooperation was requested and received from all party and government institutions involved in the implementation of the "Final Solution."

In these 12 trials, 177 Nazi criminals were tried and convicted. Of these, 12 were sentenced to death, 25 to life imprisonment, and the remainder to long prison terms. However, the Clemency Act passed in January 1951 by the U.S. high commissioner in Germany, John J. McCloy, resulted in the early liberation of the majority of the accused.

The U.S. tribunals met in 1,200 sessions, and the proceedings recorded in them cover 330,000 pages (aside from documents). This vast corpus of material supplements extensively the material from the International Military Tribunal. A large part of the documentation of the Nuremberg Military trials was published by the U.S. authorities in 15 volumes (*Trials of War Criminals*—"Green Series," 1949–53).

In the U.S. Occupation Zone (in Dachau) 1,517 of the 1,941 criminals who were tried by 1949 were found guilty. **151**

Of these, 324 were sentenced to death, and 278 of these sentences were actually carried out. In the British Occupation Zone in Lueneburg, Hamburg, and Wuppertal, 1,085 defendants were tried before the British military tribunal and 240 of them were sentenced to death. Among the important trials in the British Zone, that of the S.S. guards at the Bergen-Belsen concentration camp (Sept. 17–Nov. 17, 1945, the Bergen Trial) should be mentioned. Josef Kramer, the camp commander, and his accomplices were convicted. In the French Zone, 2,107 criminals were tried and 104 of them were sentenced to death. The sum total of Nazi criminals convicted in the three Western Occupation Zones of Germany between 1945 and 1949 was 5,025, of whom 806 were sentenced to death. In only 486 instances was the verdict carried out and the accused executed. In the remainder of the cases, the sentences were commuted to prison terms of varying lengths. Official or semi-official figures are not available for the trials of Nazis in the Soviet Occupation Zone of Germany. It is assumed, however, that tens of thousands of Germans were tried there and that most of them were convicted and in large measure deported to Soviet territories to serve their sentences. (In 1955, in the wake of a Soviet-West German agreement, 8,877 criminals were freed. Another 749 were handed over to Germany for further investigation.)

In the course of its work, the United Nations War Crimes Commission prepared 80 lists of "war criminals," which together comprise 36,529 names (including Japanese). The Commission published a number of partial statistics on the period until March 1, 1948. The authorities of the United States, Great Britain, France, Greece, Holland, Norway, Poland, and Yugoslavia conducted 969 trials, in which 3,470 German defendants were tried. Death sentences were passed for 952, 1,905 were sentenced to varying prison terms, and 613 were acquitted.

In Various Countries. Since the end of the war, many countries that had been occupied by the Nazis have conducted a large number of trials. Most of these countries tried the Nazis and their collaborators in the occupied lands in accordance with special legislation; but the number of criminals of German origin was relatively low. The reason for this stems from the fact that the Nazi criminals (except those captured) were not always found within their borders—although an extradition agreement was reached, and within its framework many hundreds of Nazi criminals were extradited to the legal authorities of the countries in which they committed crimes. The extradition activities continued only until 1950. Summarized below are several trials, held in various countries, that are of special interest from a Jewish viewpoint.

In Poland, trials were held from 1944 in accordance with special legislation for trying Nazi criminals. The special tribunals that were established functioned until 1946, during which time 2,471 defendants were convicted (out of about 10,000), 631 were sentenced to death, and the remainder were sentenced to varying prison terms. The following trials were significant in their bearing on the Holocaust: Amon Goeth, commander of the Plaszow concentration camp, 1946; Ludwig Fischer, governor of the Warsaw District, 1947; Rudolf Hoess, commander of the Auschwitz death camp, 1947; S.S. General Juergen Stroop, suppressor of the Warsaw ghetto uprising, 1951; S.S. General J. Sporrenberg, responsible for the slaughter of Jews in the Majdanek death camp, 1950. According to unofficial statistics (until 1968), the Polish tribunals dealt with about 40,000 persons accused of Nazi crimes (Germans and various collaborators).

In Czechoslovakia, the following, inter alia, were tried for crimes: Dieter Wisliceny, Eichmann's aide; Karl Frank, commander of the police and the S.S. in Czechoslovakia; and Josef Stefan Tiso, Alexander Mach, and Anton Vasek, collaborators with the Nazis among the Slovak leaders responsible for the annihilation of Jews in Slovakia, and others. According to available statistics, 19,000 persons were brought to trial in Czechoslovakia, but the vast majority were local collaborators.

In Hungary, according to official statistics of the Ministry of Justice, up to March 1, 1948, proceedings were instituted against 39,514 persons, of which 31,472 were completed and 8,042 were still pending. The courts dismissed 5,954 cases, 9,245 cases resulted in "not guilty" verdicts, and 19,273 defendants were sentenced to various prison terms. Three hundred and twenty-two persons were sentenced to death and only 149 persons were executed. No official data are available for post-1948 trials. The Blitz-Holocaust in Hungary was an important ingredient in the war-crime trials in that country. Among the minor war criminals were those of the "labor battalions" and people involved in the deportation of the Jews. As to major war criminals, the former prime minister, László Bárdossy, was held responsible for the deportation of Jews to Kamenets-Podolski and for the Novi Sad massacre; he was executed. Another former prime minister, Béla Imrédy, was charged with responsibility inter alia for the anti-Jewish laws and for the destruction of Hungarian Jewry; he, too, was executed. Three leading men of the Ministry of Interior—the minister, Andor Jaross, and the state secretaries, László Baky and László Endre, who played a leading part in the destruction of Hungarian Jewry—were sentenced to death and executed. Practically all members of the Szálasi and Sztójay governments (including the prime ministers) were tried and sentenced to death.

In Holland, most of the trials took place between 1948 and 1952. More than 200 accused collaborators were tried, as well as several Germans. Among the latter, the trials of the following should be mentioned: Hans Rauter (1948), commander of the police and S.S. in Holland; Wilhelm Harster, commander of the Security Police (SD) in Holland, who bore the chief responsibility for the deportation of Dutch Jews to the death camps; and Ferdinand aus der Fuenten (1949), Harster's aide, who was also responsible for the deportation of the Jews from Holland. Harster was brought to trial in The Hague on March 23, 1949, and sentenced to 12 years imprisonment. (He was sentenced to

Reading of the verdict at the Paris Military Tribunal which tried Karl Oberg and Helmut Knochen, October 1954.
Courtesy Yad Vashem Archives, Jerusalem.

an additonal 15 years imprisonment in another trial in Munich.) Aus der Fuenten's original death sentence was later commuted to life imprisonment.

Many trials were also held in Denmark, Belgium (610), Norway (81), and France (2,345), among them the trials of Karl Oberg and Helmut Knochen, police and S.S. commanders responsible for the deportation of French Jews to the death camps, and others. All in all, according to West German sources, about 80,000 Germans were convicted in all the countries (including the Soviet Union and East Germany) for committing crimes against humanity. The number of local collaborators reaches the tens of thousands. For example, 13,600 collaborators were tried in Denmark alone. More than 90% of all collaborators were sentenced to less than four years' imprisonment.

In spite of all their drawbacks and limitations, which resulted from the lack of time and the existing circumstances, the above trials can lay claim to notable achievements. A vast store of documentary material on the criminal policies of the Nazi regime toward the Jewish 155 population and on the responsibility of the leaders for executing the crimes was collected by the Allies. Likewise, records and collections of documents from the main trials, in various languages, were also published. In all these trials, the Jewish aspect, despite its great importance, manifested itself as only one of the many facets of the Nazi crime, all of which were required for establishing the responsibility of the accused for the various violations of international law: crimes against peace, war crimes, and crimes against humanity. In contrast, the only comprehensive trial that dealt entirely with the complete spectrum of the annihilation of the Jews—the "Final Solution"—was the Eichmann Trial held in Jerusalem (see below). The Eichmann Trial had important implications for the trials of Nazi criminals and their aides in those countries where trials against Nazi criminals were still being conducted (West and East Germany, Austria, and the U.S.S.R.).

In the Soviet Union Since 1961. In recent years trials have been held in the Soviet Union against Soviet citizens who collaborated with the Nazis in occupied territories during the war. Inasmuch as official publications and documents on these trials are not available, information about them is gleaned primarily from publications of the Soviet Information Agency, Tass. Implicated in these trials were also collaborators who were previously Soviet citizens, i.e., those who fled from the Soviet army and found asylum in the Western countries. Trials since 1961 deal explicitly with the annihilation of Jews *qua* Jews, while in trials held elsewhere in the U.S.S.R., Jews were submerged in the broad category of Soviet citizens. An important trial in which the question of Jewish annihilation and the role of Latvian collaborators in it was particularly outstanding was held in Riga, Latvia, in October 1965.

In West German and Austrian Courts. Courts in postwar Germany began to function at the end of 1945, when some of the Allies reinvested the Germans with the right to hold trials. According to a summary prepared by the Federal Department of Justice in Bonn, indictments were issued by the German authorities against 9,401 Nazi criminals between 1945 and Jan. 1, 1969. Of these, 12 were condemned to death (until 1949), 98 to life imprisonment, 6,002 to various prison terms, and the remainder were acquitted or left unpunished. All in all, during the above period investigations were carried out against 79,401 accused Nazi criminals.

Three periods are discernible in the trial and punishment of Nazi criminals in West Germany: from the close of the war until 1952, the "denazification period;" 1952–57, a period of relative cessation of legal activities in this area; and from 1958 on, with the establishment of the Central Agency of the Ministries of Justice of the States (Zentral-stelle der Landesjustizverwaltungen) in Ludwigsburg. Immediately after the end of World War II, the Allies realized that in the interests of international security, Germany must be thoroughly purged of its Nazi elements. "Denazifica-tion," purging Germany of Nazi background, which began in 1945, had several aspects: military, political, and legal. In the military sphere, they were the achievement of security conditions for the armed forces and the military govern-ments of the Allies in Occupied Germany and the prevention of any attack upon them by Nazi elements by preventive arrest of members of all Nazi government, military, police, and party bodies. In the political sphere, they covered preventing the infiltration of Nazis not included in the list of war criminals into influential positions in public, economic, and social life of Germany, in order to assure the process of German democratization. In the legal sphere, they constituted bringing the accused to trial, when the disclosures relative to their pasts justified a trial. More than 3,000,000 Germans were obliged to undergo the purging process. In accordance with these objectives, trials were conducted against Nazi criminals in both Allied and German courts. From 1946 to 1952, trials were held, inter alia, against participants in the *Kristall-nacht* riots (Nov. 9–10, 1939), and the number of accused reached several hundred.

After 1953, "denazification" ceased in West and East Germany. The preparations for searching for criminals not yet brought to trial abated, and many were able to flee Germany (e.g., to Latin America, Australia, the Arab countries, etc.), with the result that murderers were living freely and without fear throughout the world (Adolf Eichmann lived in Argentina; the physician Josef Mengele, "the monster of Auschwitz," lived in Argentina until 1960; Horst Schumann, who performed medical experiments on Jewish prisoners in the concentration camps, lived in Ghana until his extradition; Franz Stangl, the commander of the Treblinka and Sobibor death camps, lived in Brazil until his extradition, etc.). The German authorities rationalized the cessation of activities by claiming that the Nuremberg Trials, inasmuch as they were held in Germany, did not evoke the appropriate reaction in the country. After the overwhelming defeat, the German nation was busy restoring the ruins created by the war. Appropriate documentation was lacking, inasmuch as the victors took as spoils all the German archives that remained after the war. The reservoir of potential witnesses that existed in Germany between 1945 and 1950 and constituted an important element in gathering complaints and evidence against the criminals disappeared with the elimination of Displaced Persons camps in Germany and the migration of the refugees to Israel and other countries. In addition, the German people and its authorized institutions were not at all aware of the extent of the crimes committed by the Nazis. Therefore, claimed the Germans, it was only in the wake of the famous Ulm trial, held in 1958 against the members of the *Einsatzkommando Tilsit,* who operated in Lithuania, that they learned of the extent of the crimes.

Whatever the validity of this claim, it is a fact that 1958 constituted a turning point in renewed activity toward bringing Nazi criminals to justice within the territory of the German Federal Republic, and, to a far lesser extent, in Austria. In a number of places in the world, especially in West Germany, Israel (the work of Yad Vashem and the establishment of a special unit for Nazi criminals within the Israel Police Force), and the United States (where the Institute of Jewish Affairs concentrated exclusively on judicial assistance to German and Austrian authorities), suitable conditions and tools were created for renewed activity in this field. In the Ulm trial, so claim the Germans, it became clear to the prosecution that until that time the crime of the "Final Solution" of the Jews in Eastern Europe was barely considered by German courts and that those mainly responsible for its planning and execution were not tried at all.

In the wake of this trial, there was an awakening among liberal jurists in Germany. The already mentioned Zentralestelle der Landesjustizverwaltungen zur Aufklaerung der NS-Verbrechen was created 13 years after the war in the city of Ludwigsburg, near Stuttgart, during a special session of the ministers of justice of the 13 Laender constituting the Federal Republic of Germany. It convened in October 1958. The employees of the institution were general prosecutors and investigating judges; the majority were devoted young people. They began their work by becoming acquainted with the problem, gathering documentary material and establishing ties with Israel and Jewish institutions in the United States. This office did not deal with crimes committed within German territory itself; they were dealt with, according to the residential area of the accused, by the regular judicial authorities in Germany. It undertook to uncover and investigate those crimes committed beyond German boundaries, particularly in Eastern Europe. The office came up against many and complicated problems. On the one hand, its activities were an annoyance and a threat to those German circles that included many influential figures who would like to forget the past, e.g., ex-Nazi politicians, various judges and police officials, neo-Nazis circles, etc. On the other hand, it encountered many difficulties and obstacles in gathering documentary material scattered in many countries. Certain countries for political reasons were not always willing to assist by placing 159 the material in their possession at the disposal of the German authorities.

An additional stumbling block encountered by the office was the location of suitable eyewitnesses. The interrogation of witnesses from the ranks of Jewish survivors posed many difficulties, as many of them did not remember the names of those who committed the crimes. Although they were well aware of the vital importance of their testimony for the conviction of the criminals, a few refused to give testimony on the grounds that they did not want to relive the terrible past. Some of them refused to go to Germany or Austria and therefore could not testify directly before a German or Austrian court. The problem of locating witnesses intensified as the time passed and the Holocaust period receded into the past. In addition, many of the survivors were dead; some had changed their names and homes. The problem was even greater with respect to German witnesses, who were unwilling to give incriminating testimonies against their accomplices. Nevertheless, despite these and other problems, the office did important work during its years of activity. By Jan. 1, 1969, the office had undertaken 1,830 major investigations and had already given over a large part of them to the competent legal authorities. More than 60,000 suspected or accused criminals are involved in these investigations and more than 500 additional investigations had been carried out by the office by the end of 1969.

A large part of the investigations handed over for legal consideration was completed with the trial and conviction of the accused, e.g., the trials of the S.S. men from the staff of the Chelmno death camp; the members of the *Einsatzgruppen* who operated in Belorussia; the Heuser trial on the destruction of the Jews of Minsk; the trials of the murderers of the Treblinka, Auschwitz, and Sobibor death camps and the Tarnopol, Czestochowa, Lvov, and Stanislav ghettos. The office set up a central catalogue of Nazi criminals (including those who died, were freed, etc.), containing 190,000 names. Special units of the criminal

Some of the accused in the Frankfort Auschwitz trial which began on December 20, 1963, and ended on August 20, 1965.

police squad were established to assist the office; their task was to interrogate witnesses in Germany, locate criminals, and make arrests on the basis of the office's data. Among the important cases dealt with by the office are the following: the *Einsatzgruppen,* with all their units, which operated mainly in the Nazi-occupied Soviet territories;

and the infamous *Aktion* Reinhard case, the operation aimed at annihilating about 2,000,000 Polish Jews. The office also investigated the crimes committed in the ghettos in the various regions of Poland and in all Nazi-occupied countries of Europe.

Despite the proclamations and claims of government circles in Austria about the desire to eradicate traces of Nazism and anti-Semitism from the country, the acts of the Austrian courts attest the opposite. Only isolated trials against Nazi criminals were held in Austria in the 1960s, and all the verdicts constituted a mockery of justice and law, to the point of arousing wrath the world over. Among those brought to trial were: Franz Novak, a S.S. member and Eichmann's aide, who organized the transport of tens of thousands of Jews to the gas chambers; and Franz Murer, the murderer of Vilna Jewry, who was acquitted by the court in Graz, Austria, of a charge of murder and is free; Erich Raja Rajakowitsch, Eichmann's aide, who was responsible for sending tens of thousands of Dutch Jews to the death camps, was sentenced to two and a half years' imprisonment; the Mauer brothers, criminals who committed atrocities and murdered the Jews of the city of Stanislav, in Eastern Galicia (now Ukrainian S.S.R.).

Punishment of Criminals Tried in West Germany and Austria. In contrast to the period immediately after the war, when membership in a Nazi organization was sufficient for a prima facie case, according to German criminal law, it must be proven that the individual defendant committed acts of murder or was an accomplice to these acts. Although it was still possible to find Jewish eyewitnesses to testify against low-ranking Nazis, it was almost impossible to do so in the case of high-ranking officials, viz., those who gave the commands. It was only on the basis of testimony given by accomplices or documents from that period that they could be brought to trial, and these were often nonexistent. The verdicts of trials against Nazi criminals in West Germany, and even more so in Austria, often reflected the tendency to exonerate criminals from severe punishment or

162

to acquit them completely on the basis that they had committed these acts out of "an error of conscience." According to this plea, it was incumbent upon them to carry out every act that fell within the realm of their official roles, according to Nazi laws and the policy of the Nazi Party. It only had to be proven that they were faced with the choice of killing or being killed.

After the institutions involved in and outside Germany had gathered a substantial amount of material and testimony against them, many of the criminals nonetheless received a sentence that does not stand in any proportion to the extent of their crimes. Tens of thousands of other defendants enjoyed the immunity afforded by the German statute of limitations, twice extended and now 30 years in the case of murder. The reasons for this leniency included the fact that many German and Austrian judges or jurors themselves served the Nazi regime and some of the judges and jurors were members of the Nazi Party. Even those who were not Nazis were not inclined to mete out severe punishments to their neighbors. The indifference of the bulk of the German and Austrian public to the question of Nazi criminals also played a role in this matter.

Various circles in Germany and a large part of the German press have protested, more than once, against the absurdity of the light punishments or the acquittals of the criminals in comparison to punishments meted out to regular thieves, murderers, and others. In contrast, the voices of Nazi sympathizers encouraged the acquittals and the lenient sentences.

Number of Nazi Criminals and Their Collaborators. As it is not possible to establish exactly the number of German criminals who participated in the annihilation of the Jews, only an estimate is possible. There were two main groups of criminals: the instigators, the planners, and the commanders, who directed the killing operations or with whose knowledge, agreement, and passive participation these acts were committed; and the actual implementors of the plans and the commands at various levels of authority and initiative. The first group, to which the High Command of the German government belonged—the heads of the Nazi Party, the heads of the Gestapo, the S.S., and the Head Office for the Security of the Reich—numbered many hundreds. The second group included hundreds of thousands of people—members of the Gestapo, the S.S., the Waffen S.S. units, the S.D., the police with its many branches in Nazi Germany, officials from special departments of the Foreign Ministry and Ministry of the Interior who dealt with Jewish matters, the staff of the concentration camps, doctors who practiced in the concentration camps, lawyers, judges, members of the armed forces, etc. The above number of Nazi criminals who participated actively in the annihilation of the Jews is therefore no exaggeration.

This number, however, does not include the collaborators from the conquered territories—Croats, Ukrainians, Latvians, Lithuanians, Russians, etc. Tens of thousands of collaborators who participated in the planning and execution of the murder of Jews, Soviet prisoners of war, and local civilian populations, enjoyed complete freedom in their places of residence or found asylum in the United States, Latin America, Australia, the Arab countries, etc. During the war, they were organized in special units, e.g., in the Ukrainian militia, Bandera gangs, S.S. units, police, etc. They not only fulfilled the order of the Nazis, but also killed tens of thousands of Jews on their own initiative. The murder of the Jews of Kaunas and other areas in Lithuania, for example, began immediately upon the evacuation of the Soviet army from these places, even before the first German soldiers entered. The same was true in Lvov, other places in Eastern Galicia, and elsewhere.

The Lesson of the Trials. After 1958, and especially after the capture and trial of Eichmann, a change became noticeable in the punishment of Nazi criminals. In Germany and in other countries, trials were renewed against a number of Nazis who had long ceased to be under investigation; the search for Nazi criminals who had thus far succeeded in avoiding imprisonment was intensified; the possibilities for Nazis to exploit the rights of asylum in other countries were diminished; there was an increased awareness that the crimes of the Nazis must not be forgotten and that the criminals must be punished in order to prevent a recurrence of the crimes. Although the sentences meted out to Nazi criminals in most of the trials in West Germany, and especially in Austria, are in no way proportionate to the crimes (if proportion is at all possible), the careful preparation of the trials by the prosecution and the openness and the thoroughness of the substantiated verdicts, based, inter alia, on testimony given by Jews, resulted in their contributing significantly to the research of the Holocaust history for the reeducation of the German people, and especially German youth.

9 ADOLF EICHMANN AND
THE EICHMANN TRIAL

One of the most sinister figures in the Nazi hierarchy, Eichmann identified himself completely with the aims of the criminal plot to destroy the Jews and during the final stages of World War II seems to have become absolutely obsessed by them. It is not surprising that after the war he was called "the great transport officer of death." Born in Solingen, Germany, Eichmann was the oldest son of a clerk. His parents, both Protestants, moved with their family to Linz, Austria, when Eichmann was eight years old. There he attended elementary and high school and was later sent to a technical school; he did not excel in his studies. From 1928 to 1933 he worked as a traveling salesman for the Socony Vacuum Company.

Eichmann was a member of the paramilitary German-Austrian Front Fighters organization and in 1932 joined the Nazi Party. He was introduced into the party by his friend Ernst Kaltenbrunner, who became later the notorious commander of the Reich Security Head Office (R.S.H.A.). He became a member of the S.S., left Austria for the Reich, and in 1933 received his military training in one of the German S.S. camps. In 1934 he served as an S.S. corporal in the concentration camp of Dachau, his first confrontation with systematic terror and violence. At the end of the same year he volunteered for the Secret Service (S.D.) and a year later started to work in its Jewish Section. At first his employment there was mainly in the field of intelligence. He was sent to the Near East, including Palestine, and presented a detailed report of his trip. Gradually he set about acquiring a knowledge of Judaism and Jewish organizations, tried to learn some Yiddish and

Hebrew, and by 1938 had become the expert authority on Zionist organizations and Jewish emigration. At the same time, he also rose to the commissioned ranks of the S.S. With the *Anschluss* of Austria in March 1938 Eichmann was sent there to promote Jewish emigration. He devoted himself with ruthless zeal to the policy of compelling Jews to emigrate and organized the process of their expropriation and expulsion on the assembly-line principle. The center he founded in Vienna (Center for Jewish Emigration; Zentralstelle fuer juedische Auswanderung) was so successful that a similar institution was established in Prague after the German take-over of Czechoslovakia in 1939, and the same system was applied in the office of the German Center of Jewish Emigration in Berlin. In 1939 Eichmann returned to Berlin, rose to the rank of captain, and became director of the Reich Center of Jewish Emigration (Zentralstelle fuer juedische Auswanderung). After the outbreak of World War II, he engaged in the tragic expulsion of Jews to the Nisko region of Poland.

In March 1941 Eichmann was appointed head of the Gestapo's Section IVB4, which dealt with Jewish affairs and the expulsion of populations. In mid-1941 when the term "final solution of the Jewish question" received its most sinister interpretation, i.e., of the complete physical extermination of the Jewish people (see chapter 1), Himmler and Heydrich gave Eichmann complete responsibility for every aspect of this operation. It can hardly be a coincidence that while practically all the other heads of departments in the Gestapo and the other senior officials of the R.S.H.A. were periodically rotated and entrusted with other duties, Eichmann remained head of the Department for Jewish Affairs at Gestapo headquarters until the final collapse of the Third Reich. It is evident that Eichmann was wholeheartedly devoted to this gruesome assignment, for had he shown the slightest reluctance to continue he would immediately have been relieved by his superiors.

In November 1941 Eichmann was promoted to *Obersturmbannfuehrer* (lieutenant colonel), a rank which he held up to the end of the war. When the *Einsatzgruppen* began their slaughter of Soviet Jewry, he organized the deportation of Jews from Central European countries to the extermination centers in the East. At the beginning of 1942, after the Wannsee Conference (which he prepared and organized), he was given extensive powers to direct the deportations of European Jews to the death camps. He determined the pace and the timing of the deportations, and requests for the exemption of individual Jews, even when made by the highest German authorities, were decided upon, and invariably rejected by him. In Jewish matters he could pass over the heads of his nominal superiors and deal directly with Himmler and Heydrich, and after the latter's death, with Kaltenbrunner. He was responsible not only for ensuring the extermination of the Jews, but also for the spoliation of their property, planning the sterilization of people who were only partly Jews, and deceiving the outside world and hiding the true facts concerning the mass murders (the relatively less gruesome ghetto at Theresienstadt was, among others, used for that purpose and was subject to Eichmann's personal direction).

In the Reich itself, Eichmann's orders were executed by the local police headquarters, each of which had an officer for Jewish affairs who was directly answerable to him. In the occupied countries he had special envoys attached to police headquarters who belonged to his section and who had authority to deal with Jewish matters under his direction. In the satellite countries, such as Rumania, Bulgaria, Slovakia and Croatia, he worked through special representatives attached to the German embassies. They procured the deportation of the Jews with the assistance of the local authorities, who were often mislead as to the true destination of the transports. Eichmann went to Hungary in person ("the master himself," as Himmler put it) to supervise the deportation of the local Jews. He was determined to do so in the shortest time possible and with a minimum of trouble or resistance. There he used cunning and trickery in order to get as many death trains through to

Adolf Eichmann (in glass booth, flanked by policemen) at his appeal before the Israel Supreme Court in Jerusalem, May 1962. The bench consists of (left to right) Judges Sussman, Agranat, Olshan (president of the Supreme Court), Silberg, and Witkon. The court is being addressed by Eichmann's counsel, Dr. Robert Servatius (standing). Government Press Office, Tel Aviv.

Auschwitz as possible, even against the wishes of the Hungarian regent Nicolas Horthy. He also played a cat and mouse game with the Jewish leaders, including the Zionist leader Rezső Kasztner. By that time, in the summer of 1944, Eichmann appears to have become so obsessed with the supreme importance of his assignment that he was even prepared to disobey and thwart Hitler's own express orders when those orders might have resulted in the escape of a few thousand Jews to Palestine. The documents from the archives of the German Foreign Ministry, which contain proof of these facts, completely explode the theory that Eichmann was merely a small cog in a machine, obeying superior orders.

When arms, ammunition, and soldiers were desperately needed by the German army in the East and the High 169

Command was clamoring for reinforcements, Eichmann still managed to get priority for his death trains to Auschwitz. When Himmler finally ordered the discontinuation of the extermination process, Eichmann managed to organize the transportation of Jews, on foot, from Hungary to Austria under such terrible conditions that they were bound to result in death marches. Ordered by his superiors to negotiate with Jewish leaders for an exchange of "goods for blood," he did so only reluctantly, believing that this might jeopardize the complete execution of the "Final Solution." In 1944 Eichmann also visited Auschwitz in person and suggested ways and means to speed up the extermination process, so that the daily death rate could be increased from 10,000 to 12,000.

At the end of the war, Eichmann was taken prisoner, but his true identity was not discovered and he succeeded in escaping, reaching Argentina in 1950. He lived in Buenos Aires under the name of Ricardo Klement, together with his wife Vera and his three sons. A worldwide search for him ended in May 1960, when he was abducted by Israelis and flown to Israel in order to stand trial for the crimes committed by him. Eichmann's abduction caused a diplomatic incident when Argentina lodged a complaint against Israel with the UN Security Council. The Israel government expressed its regret for the violation of Argentine law by Israel citizens and this, together with the resolution condemning the act, was regarded as "appropriate reparation" to the Argentine government. The Security Council also took cognizance of the need for Eichmann to be brought to trial, in view of the enormity of the Nazis' crimes against the Jewish people. It is noteworthy that this was the first and only occasion after 1948 that Israel received the support of both the U.S. and the U.S.S.R. The dispute between the two countries was in fact settled within a few weeks.

Eichmann was tried before the Jerusalem District Court (see below), with the trial lasting from April to December 1961. He was found guilty on all the main charges brought against him and sentenced to death. The Israel Supreme Court dismissed his appeal in May 1962 and the president of Israel rejected his plea for clemency. He was hanged at the Ramleh prison, his body was cremated, and the ashes were scattered over the Mediterranean Sea. The controversy and discussion about Eichmann's real character and motivation did not end with his execution and will undoubtedly continue for a long time. Most revealing in this respect, in addition to the facts outlined above, were his own words after the war and the statements made by his former friends and associates. In 1957, while living in Argentina, he had many conversations with Willem Sassen, a Dutch Nazi journalist, that were tape-recorded, transcribed, and intended for eventual publication. In the course of these talks, he repeatedly stressed that he was not just a recipient of orders, but rather an idealist. "To be frank with you," he said, "had we killed all of them, the 10.3 million, I would be happy and say, 'All right, we managed to destroy an enemy.'" He blamed himself for not having been ruthless enough and cursed "all those interventionists" who hampered him in his work. His description to Sassen about the "magnificent way" in which the death trains rolled from Holland to Auschwitz makes spine-chilling reading.

Rudolf Hoess, the commander of Auschwitz, wrote in his autobiography shortly before he was executed in Poland that Eichmann "showed himself to be completely obsessed with the idea of destroying every single Jew he could lay his hands on." Hoess relates that he always felt ashamed of his momentary attacks of weakness, after having talked with *Obersturmbannfuehrer* Eichmann. Eichmann's associate in Section IVB4, Dieter Wisliceny, who was later hanged in Bratislava, said that "Eichmann was very cynical in his attitude to the Jewish question. He gave no indication of any human feeling toward these people. He was not immoral; he was amoral and completely ice-cold in his attitude." It was Wisliceny who described Eichmann's last address to his men before the end of the war, when he heard 171 him exclaim: "I shall leap into my grave laughing, because the feeling that I have the deaths of five million people on my conscience will be for me a source of extraordinary satisfaction." About ten years before Eichmann's trial, Bernhard Loeserer, a senior official in the Nazi Ministry of Interior, best summed up all there is to be said of this man when he wrote of Eichmann that of all the people he knew, "next to Heydrich, his chief, he was the strongest personification of satanic principles."

Eichmann Trial. The trial of Eichmann, which took place in Jerusalem in 1961, aroused immense interest all over the world and gave rise to discussions on a variety of topics: factual, legal, political, religious, and psychological. After being brought to Israel from Argentina in May 1960, Eichmann was handed over by his abductors to the police, who duly detained him and obtained from an Israel judge a warrant for his arrest, which was later extended from time to time. The pretrial investigation, which was carried out by "Bureau 06," a police unit especially set up for this purpose, lasted almost a year. Under the indictment, which was then filed by Israel attorney-general Gideon Hausner, who headed the prosecution team, Eichmann was charged with "crimes against the Jewish people . . . crimes against humanity . . . war-crimes, and membership in an 'enemy organization,' " i.e., one that had been declared a "criminal organization" by a judgment of the International Military Tribunal trying the major war criminals. All the above-mentioned crimes are offenses under the Nazi and Nazi Collaborators (Punishment) Law, which had been passed by the Knesset in 1950.

The trial before the Jerusalem District Court, presided over by Supreme Court Justice Moshe Landau, and also composed of Justices Benjamin Halevi, president of the Jerusalem District Court, and Yiẓḥak Raveh of the Tel Aviv District Court, lasted from April to December 1961. Eichmann was defended by Dr. Robert Servatius, a German lawyer from Cologne who had represented some of the war criminals at the Nuremberg Trials. At the beginning of the trial, counsel for defense challenged the jurisdiction of the court on a number of grounds, the most important of which were that the law under which Eichmann was charged was invalid, as it referred to acts committed outside the territorial jurisdiction of Israel and before the law had been passed, and even before the State of Israel had come into existence; that the court should not exercise its jurisdiction, as the accused had been brought within the jurisdiction without his consent, having been abducted illegally from Argentina; and that Israel judges, being Jews and therefore feeling affinity with the victims of the crimes with which Eichmann was charged, were incapable of giving him a manifestly fair trial.

The Court rejected all these arguments, holding inter alia that as the International Military Tribunal in Nuremberg had already held, crimes against humanity and war crimes were merely declaratory of existing law. Similarly, the Israel law applied had not invented new offenses in regard to acts that could have been considered as "legal" by the perpetrators at the time of their commission. The law merely enabled the courts to punish offenders for acts that have always universally been regarded as criminal, but for which the offenders could not be tried otherwise only because of the lawlessness existing in Germany during the Nazi regime. The rules concerning retroactive or extraterritorial laws were not rules of law, but rules of justice, and justice demanded that crimes of this nature should not go unpunished. An Israel court could assume jurisdiction in this case as there existed a link between the State of Israel and the "crime against the Jewish people," as defined by the law. The plan of extermination included Jews living at that time in Palestine and was one of the causes of the establishment of the state. It was irrelevant that the State of Israel did not exist at the date on which the crimes were committed. The survivors of the Jewish people were now in a position, through the sovereign State of Israel, to bring to justice the murderers who had been responsible for the massacre. As to the argument concerning Eichmann's 173 abduction, the court held, relying on numerous decisions by British and U.S. Courts, that a person who is brought before a court in order to be tried for an offense against the laws of the state to which that court belongs may not oppose his trial by reason of the illegality of his arrest or of the means whereby he was brought within the jurisdiction of that state. As to the emotional involvement of the judges, the court stated that a judge, when dispensing justice, does not cease to be a human being with human emotions and passions, but a professional judge can and must overcome those feelings, otherwise no judge would ever be fit to try a criminal case that evoked deep feelings and revulsion, like treason or murder.

After the dismissal of the preliminary objections of the defense, the full drama and tragedy of the Holocaust were unfolded. With the help of more than a hundred witnesses and some 1,600 documents, mostly taken from German archives, all the aspects of the Nazi persecution of the Jews, from the initial anti-Jewish legislation to the systematic attempts to exterminate the whole of European Jewry, as well as the part which the accused had played in the execution of every stage of the criminal scheme (see chap. 1), were depicted before the court. Most of the facts were not disputed by the defense, but Eichmann tried consistently to minimize the role he had played, claiming that he had merely been a "small cog" in the machine and had been bound by his oath of allegiance to obey all the orders given to him. He attempted to shift a major part of the responsibility onto his superiors and subordinates alike.

The court did not accept Eichmann's version in this regard and found that he had been a central figure in carrying out every stage of the "Final Solution." He had acted out of hatred for the Jews and a desire for their annihilation. He could not rely on the argument that he had merely carried out "superior orders," which in law did not constitute a valid defense for manifest crimes, as he had done everything in his power to interpret and execute the orders he had received in the most extreme and uncompromising way and had even exceeded the duties imposed upon him. Consequently he was convicted by the court of all charges in the indictment with some minor amendments, and sentenced to death. The case was reviewed on appeal by five judges of the Israel Supreme Court, headed by its president, Y. Olshan, who in May 1962 decided to dismiss Eichmann's appeal. After the rejection of a plea for clemency by the president of Israel, Eichmann was executed.

The whole story of the capture and trial of Eichmann captured the world's imagination and was widely followed in its projection over the mass media. There was widespread sympathy for Israel's actions and appreciation for the conduct of the trial, but dissident cries were also heard on the lines of the above-mentioned issues raised by the counsel for the defense. In the later stages there were appeals to Israel to show magnanimity by not inflicting the death sentence. Among the voices in this direction were some Jews (e.g., Victor Gollancz[21]). But it was clear that the bulk of public opinion sympathized with Israel's action, and as the trial proceeded, its revelations produced a renewed revulsion against the Nazis and against Eichmann who was seen as its epitome. Those responsible for holding the trial in Israel saw it not only as an act of justice but also as an educational factor—especially for the new generation both abroad and in Israel which after a lapse of only 15 years was already failing to grasp the immensity and implications of the Holocaust. In Germany a new impetus was given to the conduct of trials against Nazi criminals. Questions were asked by young and old as to the conditions that made the commission of such horrifying crimes possible and the reason for the rest of the world's failure to prevent them. The behavior of the Jewish leaders was subjected to close scrutiny and controversy, and the reasons for the victims' initial inability to resist were, perhaps for the first time, fully understood, even by Israel's younger generation. At the

[21] British publisher and author

Eichmann trial, for once, the Nazi "Final Solution of the Jewish Question" constituted the focal point of a serious, juridical examination and thereby gave rise to an awareness of the Holocaust, which until then, had been largely absent. The trial had also given new stimulus to Holocaust research.

10 SOVIET RUSSIA AND
THE HOLOCAUST

After Stalin's rapprochement with Nazi Germany, which became formalized in August 1939 in the Ribbentrop–Molotov pact, Soviet diplomacy, press, and propaganda underplayed and ultimately concealed the persecutions of Jews by the Third Reich, which from September 1939 turned into outright atrocities in the occupied Polish territories. Thus, Soviet Jews were not forewarned about the anti-Jewish extermination system when they came under German occupation. However, after the German attack on the U.S.S.R. (June 1941) and until the end of World War II (1945) Soviet diplomacy and propaganda stressed the barbarian character of Nazism, sometimes—as in a diplomatic note signed by V. Molotov in January 1942 —even pointing out that many of the victims were "Jews, including women and children of all ages." The formation of the Jewish Anti-Fascist Committee (in 1941–42) also served to exploit in the West the feelings of Soviet Jewish solidarity against the common Nazi enemy. Even in internal Soviet press reports, in which Ilya Ehrenburg played an important role as a war correspondent attached to the Soviet army advancing into previously German-occupied territory, the Jewish aspect of the Nazi atrocities was mentioned and sometimes vividly described.

But almost immediately after the war a complete change of "line" was imposed in this respect, apparently by Stalin himself, who adjusted his policy to the saying "Hitlers come and go, but the German people will remain forever." This adjustment brought about a renewed suppression of any information on the systematic extermination of the Jews in the German-occupied parts of the Soviet Union.

The publication of the Black Book on these atrocities, edited by I. Ehrenburg and compiled, mainly from eye-witness reports, by the Soviet Jewish writer Vasili Grossman, was at the last moment prohibited by Stalin's censorship. N. S. Khrushchev, who at the time was in charge of the administration of the Ukraine, came to the conclusion that this policy of suppressing the truth about the Jews was imperative. A large segment of the local population, whom he decided not to antagonize, had actively or passively helped the Nazis in the mass-killing of Jews. Moreover he would or could not impose on them the restoration of housing, jobs, and positions to the surviving Jews returning to the Ukraine. Throughout the Khrushchev regime (1953-64) and also under his successors this line of suppressing the truth was consistently implemented in the U.S.S.R. as a whole. When, during the "thaw" of de-Stalinization, a different tone could sometimes be voiced by intellectuals (as, e.g., Victor Nekrasov's public demand in 1959 for the erection of a memorial in Babi Yar, or Yevgeni Yev-tushenko's poem "Babi Yar" in 1961), an immediate counter-offensive with anti-Semitic overtones was launched by the official literary establishment, culminating in 1963 in a public outburst against Yevtushenko by Khrushchev himself. The throwing of the extermination of Jews into the Soviet "memory hole" went so far that the erection of monuments on Jewish mass-graves was prevented, or at least the specific mention of Jews as victims was omitted. Where such memorials or inscriptions already existed, as in Vilna or Kovno (Kaunas), they were destroyed or ob-literated and sometimes replaced by the "neutral" formula (also used in the press, in literature, and in historiography) about the victims of the Nazi mass-extermination having been "innocent Soviet citizens" or "Russians, Ukrainians, and others." (The known exceptions to this rule are an early memorial-stone with a Yiddish inscription near Minsk and the Yiddish translation of the neutral "victims-of-fascism"-formula on a memorial in a forest near Riga.)

178 Krushchev publicly stressed that the Soviet Jews

under Nazi occupation were "like everybody else, good and bad," some of them having cooperated with the Nazis against the Soviets.

After the 1967 Israel-Arab Six-Day War, this line was intensified, assuming an absurd and even obscene character. In conjunction with the unleashing of the "anti-Zionist" hate-campaign, Soviet propaganda began to repeat the formula that the millions of Jews exterminated during the Holocaust were in fact the victims of "Zionist-Nazi co-operation." All kinds of publications elaborated and "documented" the thesis of a "Zionist-Nazi conspiracy," which included the mass-killing of Jews. This new turn was apparently meant to serve the momentary political purpose of presenting the State of Israel as "the Nazis of our time" and the "enemy of progressive mankind."

The emotional reaction of Soviet Jews to this official policy and propaganda, both on the Holocaust and on "Nazi" Israel, was a very potent factor in stimulating the neo-Zionist wave among them, even in completely assimilated circles.

11 ARAB ATTITUDES
   TO THE HOLOCAUST

It is hardly possible to sum up what was the prevalent attitude in Arab societies when the news about the Holocaust spread in the world. But it is significant that in Arab writings and declarations by leaders it has been repeatedly argued that Germany's actions were justified because of the evil the Jews did to her and the danger they constituted to the country! These actions, it is explained, were necessary for self-defense. A few examples:

Abdallah al-Tall[22] denounces the Jewish slander *(firya)* against the Nazis. Realizing that the Jews were the cause of their defeat in World War I, the Germans, he says, were afraid they might bring about a second defeat in World War II—"and this is what happened." Hitler has been "wronged and slandered," for he did no more to the Jews than Pharaoh, Nebuchadnezzar, the Romans, the Byzantines, Titus, Muhammad, and the European peoples who slaughtered the Jews before him. The crimes and barbarities of the Jews, founded on the Talmud and the *Protocols*, the sucking of human blood, poisoning of wells, Freemasonry, have not changed. Hitler appointed a committee of scholars, who reached the conclusion that the Jews must be liquidated or expelled:

Hitler carried out the decision of his scholars, and did to the Jews as has been done unto them throughout the generations—killing, burning, and expulsion from the countries which they betrayed and whose peoples they deceived *(Khaṭir al-Yahūdiyya al-*

<hr />

[22] Arab soldier, commander of the Arab Legion in the War of Independence and presently senator in the Jordanian senate.

'Ālamiyya 'Alā al-Islām wa-al-Masihiyya ("The Danger of World Jewry to Islam and Christianity"), 115-7).

Tall adds, indeed (pp. 119-20), that he does not want the reader to think that he agrees with the slaughter of the Jews, for nothing could be further from the minds of the Arabs than the idea of massacre. He recalls the events of the past only because they confirm the evil character of the Jews and their foul customs, and he regrets that the Arabs have to suffer for the sufferings of the Jews at the hands of the Germans. In another passage he explains:

The blame [for the massacre of the Jews] applies first and fore-most to the Jews themselves and their characteristics of treachery *(ghadr)*, deceitfulness *(makr)*, crime and treason, and in the second place to European civilization, which apparently could not long suffer the vile *(maqit)* Jewish character, and in the course of time hatred of the Jews and loathing for their vices led to a movement of collective killing (p. 283).

Muhammad Ali 'Aluba's[23] attitude is similar. After enumerating the evil deeds of the Jews, he continues:

This is what led Hitler to alarm the world against them, not because he was a believer and feared God, but because he wanted to save his nation and the world from this malignant evil that had permeated the Christian peoples, and the poison that flowed in the bodies of the non-Jews. It is well known that the German people is one of the most progressive in the world in science, technology, and nationalism, and it has an immunity which can defend it against the activities of Zionism. Nevertheless, Hitler realized what was weakening his people to the extent that it almost brought about its end. The same applies with greater force to other nations, which are not so immune (*Filasṭīn wa-al-Damīr al-Insānī* ("Palestine and the Conscience of Mankind"), 176).

These arguments imply not only an attempt to explain, understand, and justify the acts of the Germans against the Jews, but also, it seems, a readiness to learn from the

[23] Egyptian statesman

Nazis. Dr. Muhammad Abd al-Muʿizz Naṣr[24] writes:

The truth is that the study of what Hitler wrote on world Zionism has become a vital matter for anyone who lives in the Arab countries after the year 1948 (al-Ṣahyūniyya fī al-Majāl al-Dawli ("Zionism in International Affairs"), 87).

It is repeatedly argued that the Germans did not really exterminate six million Jews, and that the Jews and Israel exaggerate the dimensions of the Holocaust in order to derive political advantages from it. They pretend to be persecuted for the purpose of extorting compassion; other peoples were also injured by the Nazis, but only the Jews trade in their sufferings. In a talk with Dr. Frei, editor of the German neo-Nazi journal *Deutsche Soldaten and National Zeitung*, President Nasser is quoted as saying:

No one, even the simplest of men, takes seriously the lie about six million Jews who were murdered. How is it with you?

Dr. Frei replied:

No one denies the fact of the murder of the Jews as such, and every man of feeling deplores it deeply (May 1, 1964).

In a speech on March 8, 1965, Nasser declared:

They say that in World War II the Jews suffered from Germany. Was it only the Jews who suffered from Germany? The Czechs suffered from her, the Yugoslavs suffered, the French suffered.

Saʿad Jumʿa, in 1967 Jordan's prime minister and subsequently ambassador in London, described the destruction of six million Jews by the Nazis as a "fable legend" (*Almnamara wa Maʿarakat al Masir* ("The Conspiracy and the Battle of Destiny," Beirut 1968), 20–22).

[24] Author of "Zionism in International Affairs", 1957

Ahmad Balia al-Din[25] explains the Jewish "technique":

The Hitlerite regime destroyed more Soviet atheists, Polish Catholics, and Orthodox members of the Balkan peoples than it did Jews. But all the accounts of these massacres have been closed and settled, except for the account of the Jews, which has remained open, for there is someone who keeps up its continuous exploitation into a complex which must be atoned for with reparations and aid (*Isrāʿīliyyāt* ("Judaica"), 226).

These attempts to belittle the importance of the Holocaust are motivated, it seems, by the consideration that some support for Israel stems from an admission of the world's share in the responsibility for the extermination of European Jewry, or at least by serious disquiet on the subject. It therefore becomes an Arab interest to minimize the dimensions of the Holocaust, with the implication that the world owes nothing to the Jews. Thus the Holocaust is used to condemn the Jews for allegedly trying to collect humanity's debt to them "with interest."

[25] Egyptian leftist journalist, past President of Egyptian Association of Journalists

12 HISTORIOGRAPHY
OF THE HOLOCAUST

Jewish historiography of the Holocaust actually started during the period of the persecutions. In the communities, in the ghettos, and even in the camps, wherever Jews lived, struggled, and suffered under the Nazi rule, they tried to preserve evidence of their plight. German and Jewish documents, reports, and diaries were assembled and hidden in walls, cellars, or the ground, or left in the hands of trusted persons. Some of these caches were detected after the war by survivors, some came to light by chance, among them writings that had not even been concealed such as Anne Frank's diary which her father found among the rubble of their hiding place.

The most concentrated effort was made by the historian Emanuel Ringelblum in the Warsaw ghetto. He combined activity in relief work and mutual assistance among the Jews with the collection of documents, reports, summaries, research work, memoirs, diaries, and literature. Most noteworthy is the collection of clandestine newspapers in various languages. Under the code name "Oneg Shabbat" (literally: "Enjoyment of the Sabbath") dozens of dedicated workers assembled source material, unmatched in quantity and quality. Only about two-thirds of the containers in which it was buried were recovered after the war from the ruins of the ghetto. This material is the main source for research into the history of Polish Jewry under Nazi occupation, including Ringelblum's own writings from that period. He himself escaped from the ghetto at the time of its destruction, but in March 1944 he was discovered by the Gestapo in his hiding place in Warsaw and killed together with his family.

Men, women, and even youngsters, fighting for survival and despairing of their own chances, tried to keep alive at least the memory of what they had undergone. This activity can be understood only as stemming from their deep belief that should they perish, the Jewish people would survive. Beside this hope, aroused mainly by the national home in Palestine, they were convinced that the world at large ought to know the truth they were witnessing.

This legacy was taken up and carried on by groups of survivors in liberated Poland who founded historical societies which eventually were coordinated in the Central Jewish Historical Commission. This became the nucleus of the Jewish Historical Institute in Warsaw, the only institution in the Eastern bloc that undertook to deal with the history of the Jews under Nazi rule. Under the director Bernard (Berl) Mark (from 1949 until his death in 1966) documents and studies were published in books and periodicals, both in Yiddish and in Polish. Contact was established with institutions in other countries, including Israel. When Poland embarked in 1968 on its anti-Jewish course, most of the Institute's Jewish researchers emigrated to Israel.

One of the early initiators and organizers of these activities was the historian Philip Friedman; when he went to the West in 1946 he took with him part of the assembled material. The Commission's work at that time was continued by some of those Jews who streamed into the American zone of occupation in Germany, the so-called "Displaced Persons." The material was later transferred to the State of Israel and became part of its central Remembrance Authority (Yad Vashem) archives. Philip Friedman, who lived later in the United States, became one of the founders of the scientific historical research of the Holocaust period, dealing with bibliography, methodology, publishing sources, and writings on the different aspects of Jewish life and death.

Friedman was outstanding in his capacity to come to clear conclusions at this early date. For a decade and more after the end of the war the main Jewish activity, as far as the history of the Holocaust is concerned, was directed to collection and detection of evidence and source material, Jewish and non-Jewish. This trend was very much influenced by the event that made the decisive impact on the study of World War II for many years to come: the Nuremberg trials. The material amassed for these and the subsequent war crimes trials was so enormous in its amount and so overwhelming in the evidence it produced that scores of historians—old and new, professional and self-styled—could not exhaust it. Even today, after much additional material has come to light and state archives have been opened, the transcripts of these and subsequent trials are considered to be among the best historical sources available. In some cases, as for instance in the German Auschwitz trial (Frankfort 1963–65), the assembled documentation is of much greater significance than the judgments. It was therefore natural that the first comprehensive studies of the Holocaust period relied almost exclusively on the material of the international military tribunals. Since the origin of these sources was mostly German or from other nations involved but definitely not Jewish, the image of the Jews and their behavior was very one-sided. Mostly they were pictured as the helpless and senseless victims of the Nazi mania. If anything new became the subject of extensive research, it was this anti-Semitism. Starting already in the late thirties, countless studies probed into its history, its sociological, psychological, and political roots in order to explain what—especially after Auschwitz —seemed inexplicable. The development and implementation of what the Germans called "the final solution of the Jewish problem" was first described in the comprehensive books of Reitlinger (1953), Tennenbaum (1956), and Hilberg (1961), all of them relying heavily on the material of the Nuremberg trials.

In the meantime there developed archives and institutions making it their task to study the events that engulfed Europe's Jews under Hitler's rule. For some of the institutes studying National Socialism and the War, like those in Germany and the one in Holland, the Jewish aspect was part of their endeavor, while the Jewish ones were mainly erected for just that purpose. The Jewish Contemporary Documentation Center (C.D.J.C.) in France had been founded clandestinely in Grenoble in 1943. Its founder and director was Isaac Schneerson. After the liberation of France the C.D.J.C. was transferred to Paris and moved in 1956 to the building housing a memorial to the Unknown Jewish Martyr, erected upon the initiative of Schneerson. By the time he died in 1969, the institute had published 42 volumes of documents, studies, and monographs in addition to a quarterly *Le Monde Juif; la Revue du C. D. J. C.* The Wiener Library in London, named after its founder Alfred Wiener, is also an offspring of earlier institutions. Its predecessor was a clandestine Jewish archive in Germany collecting material about National Socialism which had to be destroyed with Hitler's access to power. It was refounded in 1934 in Amsterdam and transferred in 1939 to London where it developed into one of the best documental institutions dealing with the period, and later under Walter Laqueur, with contemporary history in general. The YIVO Institute for Jewish Research was the principal world organization conducting research in Yiddish (the abbreviation YIVO stands for "Scientific Yiddish Organization") with its headquarters in Vilna. During the Nazi occupation this institute had amassed a library of over 100,000 books and as many manuscripts and archival items, all of which were carried away by the Germans. Most of it was rediscovered and is today located in the YIVO Institute in New York. Under the leadership of Philip Friedman and Jacob Robinson—today the Nestor of Jewish research into the Holocaust—the Institute undertook joint research projects with Yad Vashem.

Yad Vashem, Martyrs' and Heroes Remembrance Authority, is the State of Israel's national institution. It was inaugurated by law in 1954 while the veteran Jewish historian, Benzion Dinur, was Minister of Education and

Culture. The legislator charged Yad Vashem (the name is derived from Isaiah 56:5) with a twofold task: to preserve the memory of the murdered, and to gather all material available about the Jewish life that had been destroyed and "regarding all those Jewish people who laid down their lives, who fought and rebelled against the Nazi enemy and their collaborators." In conscious contrast to the Jews' image as helpless victims, here there was a conscious emphasis on resistance. In accordance with this double charge, a memorial hall, a synagogue, and a permanent exhibition were erected, connected with a vast square, where on Israel's official Holocaust Remembrance Day, which is the anniversary of the Warsaw uprising, the central memorial ceremony is held. Throughout the year thousands of people, Israelis and tourists, visit the site. According to its historiographic task a library and archives have been set up, and research work and publication of books and periodicals have been undertaken. Close connections are kept up with similar institutions abroad as with law courts conducting war crimes trials. Besides this central institute, there are two others in Israel, founded by ghetto fighters and partisans who survived. Ghetto Fighters' House, which bears the name of one of the victims of the Holocaust, the great Jewish poet Itzhak Katznelson, serves as a memorial, research, documentation, and instruction center. Its museum contains a complete model of the Treblinka death camp. It publishes books, mostly memoirs from its archives, and periodicals. A similar institution is Moreshet ("heritage"), whose periodical is of special repute. Of the wealth of source material, memoirs, studies, and monographs which have been published in Israel in Hebrew, only a small part has been translated.

It has not been easy for the Jewish historian in general, and the Israeli in particular, to find the scientific research method and the spiritual equilibrium to deal with the unique tragedy of the Jewish people. This is probably the main reason why research developed rather hesitatingly. The great breakthrough came with the 1961 Eichmann trial (see chap. 9) for which the rich archives of Yad Vashem were for the first time used on a large scale. But the trial did more. It established a new consciousness, a more objective and also rational approach, and at the same time discharged much of the accumulated emotions and strain, a mixture of scorn, guilt-feelings, and recoiling. Now the catastrophe had to be faced but it also could be faced, since for the first time the Jews were in the position to deliver judgment.

Following the trial something like a public moral eruption occurred, which focused on two targets. The inner-Jewish discussion concentrated on the Jewish Council, the *Judenrat,* which the Nazis had installed everywhere for their own convenience. They were accused of collaboration in the destruction process. On the other side, more or less at the same time, Rolf Hochhuth's play *The Deputy* called the Catholic church, and especially the Pope, to account for not having intervened and protested openly against what was known all too well. The heated discussion showed that there prevailed a remarkable ignorance as to the historical facts and circumstances. This acted as a stimulant to research. Other culprits were detected. Almost simultaneously three studies appeared in the U.S. and England putting the blame on the Allies, who had not been willing to rescue the Jews. In Israel research was systematized, methods were clarified, the universities engaged in research and instruction. The rich arsenal of Jewish source material has been cataloged and made accessible. The new *Encyclopaedia Judaica* already profited from this advancing scholarship. In the U.S. there has now appeared the first general systematic and objective record of the activities of the Jewish councils, a project in which Yad Vashem and YIVO cooperated. The World Federation of Hungarian Jews published documents and studies by historians in the U.S., Israel, and Hungary. Monographs about Holland, Denmark, and Slovakia give a more complete and detailed picture. Gradually there is emerging a new school of Jewish research, whose future center is Israel. This seems to be quite natural, since the greatest amount of accessible source material is concentrated here, and the urge to come to grips with this recent catastrophic history of the Jews is vividly felt.

The relationship of the world at large to the Holocaust is mirrored in several public phenomena. Research in general and historiography in particular are part of it. Auschwitz became a catchword for human uneasiness in the Western world. The fact that a highly cultured people like the Germans could use modern technology and bureaucracy for mass murder set sociologists and psychologists, together with historians, on the path of investigation into man's nature and the human condition. For this school of thinking the destruction of the Jews serves as an example and a warning. In historiography it serves as a proof for National Socialism's innermost nature and motivates the need to take a moral stand. As Robert Cole put it: "If the history of the Nazi epoch could be explored without reference to the death camps, for example, would this not invalidate all moral judgments on the period?" This argument is brought up against A.J.P. Taylor's view of history, which sees in Hitler a traditional German statesman, and argues that the results of his policy were accidental and in the greater part provoked by the politics of the Western powers. The same discussion about Germany's guilt arose also in Germany itself. Still, there too the "final solution" has been increasingly recognized as an integral, and even the most consistent, part of Hitler's politics. Generally, very serious research has been done in Germany, partly in connection with the trials and partly independently, into facts and motives. The revelation of the German atrocities caused a shock which contributed to a revulsion from anti-Semitism and to support for the establishment of the independent State of Israel. Since then 25 years have elapsed, and a new generation often looks differently on the events of World War II giving its own interpretation of current events independently from these historical events. Israel thus feels all the more the need to keep the record straight.

13 JEWISH CONSCIOUSNESS
AFTER THE HOLOCAUST

The two major events in Jewish life in the 20th century are the Holocaust and the establishment of the State of Israel. It is impossible from both the factual and the spiritual viewpoint to separate the two. They are interdependent. Had the Jewish state come into being before Hitler and World War II, Jews would probably have also suffered great losses but these would not have developed into such a catastrophe. Had there not been Auschwitz and all it stands for, the urgent need for Jewish statehood would not have been made so categorically clear to Jews and non-Jews. It is much too early for the present generation to come to clear conclusions as to the historical as well as the spiritual consequences of these two revolutionary events which changed the course of the two thousand year history of the Jewish dispersion.

Clearly "the post-Holocaust world is fundamentally different from the previous world" (*Judaism*, 16, no. 3 (1967), 268). After Auschwitz—as in confrontation with the State of Israel—Jewish identity has to be conceived anew. Basically the modern Jew's problem is an existential one. It is the question of his being and not of his thinking. During the Holocaust, Jewish existence as such was at stake. The author and Holocaust survivor Elie Wiesel speaks about the totality of the experience and the universality of the failure—of all men, including the Jews themselves. "Everybody concerned was totally committed to his condition: the murderer to his crime, the victim to his fate, the by-stander to his indifference." And: "Never before have so many Jews been abandoned by so many Jews" (*Judaism*, *loc. cit.*, 281-2). This extreme experience poses the question: "By what values are we to act among ourselves and in relationship to the world at large in future?" This question has been called "the post-Holocaust future." But the Holocaust has aroused the even more radical question: "Where is God?" (Ignaz Maybaum). As Elie Wiesel points out: "It [the Holocaust] can be explained neither with God nor without him." To him it seems that for the first time in Jewish history the covenant was broken—this is theodicy in the extreme.

According to the Orthodox Jew, whose life is regulated by the Torah, history is the work of God. But even if we accept the Orthodox concept (as explained by Uriel Tal) that judgment, reward, and punishment are the forming principles in history, how can the murder of a million and a half Jewish children be justified even according to this concept? Yehuda Bauer denies this possibility and with it the existence of God. Answering him Eliezer Schweid wants to separate God from history, arguing that in history man's autonomous decisions become manifested, only the consequences of these decisions being determined by God. Moreover, faith, as agnosticism, is a basic condition of the human soul that is not influenced by personal or historical experiences, therefore the question of theodicy after the Holocaust is not relevant. Among the religiously inclined who are not observant but of mystical tendencies, Martin Buber tried to solve the insoluble question by speaking, in a similar way, of an "eclipse of God." Elie Wiesel was joined by Emil Fackenheim in the reaffirmation of the traditional God of their people in spite of the Holocaust. Fackenheim argued that to reject the traditional God was "to give Hitler the victory" (The Christian Century, May 6, 1970).

The secular Jew's self-understanding, especially in Israel, is rooted in his historical consciousness. "This consciousness focuses on biblical antiquity . . . but perhaps equally so this historical consciousness is focused on the Holocaust" (Uriel Tal). Here the question becomes also the universal one of modern man, his society, and his morality. Man's universal failure at Auschwitz was as much political as it was spiritual. How do we reckon with this human evil in our factual and spiritual life? The answer of Hannah Arendt, who tried to stress what she called its "banality," seems to be of no avail. It remains an open question.

This question was also not answered by the Christian Churches. Protestants as well as Catholics tried to come to grips with the part played by the Christian heritage in Nazi anti-Semitism. The Second Vatican Council, called on the initiative of Pope John XXIII, formulated in its declaration new and more tolerant principles regarding the Church's relation to non-Christian religions in general and to Judaism in particular. But, in spite of this and other ecumenical trends, Christian anti-Judaism as secular and political anti-Semitism is not a thing of the past. Jewish autonomous statehood, defying Church thinking about the Jews' dispersion as a punishment, is only slowly taken in. Jews are conscious of the fact that in the changing modern world, their old problems, which were pursued to extremes in the Holocaust, are still not solved. "We must first face up and respond to our Jewish singled-out condition"—says Fackenheim. He indicates two responses to the present Jewish crisis: "first, a commitment to Jewish survival; second, a commitment to Jewish unity." These thoughts were expressed at the end of March, 1967. During the crisis preceding the Six-Day War, these two commitments turned into reality. A unified will for survival engulfed Jews all over the world. The consciousness that Israel was standing for the universal survival of the Jewish people was part of its unwavering readiness to fight. Knowledge of the Holocaust was at the back of the mind of many young soldiers. They spoke about it after the war. "It's true that people believed that we would be exterminated if we lost the war. . . . We got this idea—or inherited it—from the concentration camps. It is a concrete idea for anyone who has grown up in Israel, even if he personally didn't experience Hitler's persecution . . . This is the lesson of the gas chambers" (*The Seventh Day*, (1970), 181).

The world of the Holocaust—says George Steiner—is "extraterritorial to reason," and he quotes Elie Wiesel: "I who was there still do not understand" (*Encounter* (Feb. 1967), 38–9). He thinks that because we are so far from understanding, we should perhaps keep silent. But: "The next best is ... to keep faith with what may well be the utopian commitment to reason and historical analysis." Gershom Scholem deals with the different and opposite kind of reaction, the commitment to mysticism. "The Jews have passed through the Holocaust and a crisis which normal human speech is powerless to describe." He warns against unseemly haste in expecting immediate results from crisis. Kabbalah and Ḥassidism were such—belated—reactions to "a tremendous upheaval in the life of the nation. ... Apparently it takes some while for the impact of history to reach those creative depths from which such movements arise." A reaction to the profound shock of the Holocaust could be either deadly or productive. "We hope it will be productive: that is why we are living here, in this Land" (*Ariel*, no. 26 (1970), 45/6).

14 SOURCES AND LITERATURE

(1) SOURCES: Primary sources of the Holocaust (official and unofficial), including some pre- and post-Holocaust material, constitute part of the archives of involved parties: Nazi Germany and occupied or controlled areas, the Allied anti-Axis coalition and the neutrals—governments-in-exile, ruling parties, armies, and peoples—as well as the Jews—the victims, those in Allied countries, and those in neutral areas. The magnitude of this documentation is obvious. Unfortunately, little of the available material is at the disposal of the researcher. Indeed, an irony exists in the fact that German sources, which are incomplete and sometimes deficient due to wanton destruction and the devastations of war, became public property, while the archives of the Allied powers and the neutrals remain largely closed, or only selectively published. Among the German documents, the most important are contained in the records of the trials from Nuremberg to Berlin, which span a 25-year period (1946–1970, and thereafter).

The most serious gap in the historiography of the Holocaust is that of the individual Jewish communities, particularly in the U.S.S.R. (October 1939 boundaries), which results from a lack of records from Allied and neutral sources. The existence of untapped rich material of Soviet and German origin in the U.S.S.R. has been established, but the documentation has not been examined thus far. For repositories of trial records, see chapter 8. Jewish material hidden during the war and gradually appearing is listed in the bibliographies.

(2) COMPREHENSIVE WORKS: G. Reitlinger, *Final Solution*... (1968²); N. Levin, *The Holocaust* (1968); H.

Krausnick, *The Anatomy of the SS-State* (1968), 1–124; R. Hilberg, *Destruction of European Jews* (1967); R. Manvell and H. Fraenkel, *The Incomparable Crime* (1967); G. Hausner, *Justice in Jerusalem* (1966), 53–261; *Algemeyne Entsiklopedye Yidn,* 6 (1963); 7 (1966); R. M. W. Kempner, *Eichmann und Komplizen* (1961; *Ha-Mikẓo'a Hashmadah; Darko shel Eichmann,* 1964); A. Eisenbach, *Hitlerowska polityka Zagłady Żydów* (1961; Yiddish version: *Di Hitleristishe Politik fun Yidn-Farnikhtung,* 1955); J. Tenenbaum, *Race and Reich* (1956; *Malkhut ha-Geza ve-ha-Resha,* 1960); L. Poliakov, *Harvest of Hate* (1954).

(3) BIBLIOGRAPHIES: Shunami, Bibl, 441–52; Bibliographical Series of Yad Vashem–YIVO: vol. 1: J. Robinson and P. Friedman, *Guide to Jewish History under Nazi Impact* (1960); vol. 2: P. Friedman, *Bibliography of Books in Hebrew on the Jewish Catastrophe and Heroism in Europe* (1960); vol. 3: P. Friedman and J. Gar, *Bibliography of Yiddish Books on the Catastrophe and Heroism* (1962); vol. 4: R. L. Braham, *Hungarian Jewish Catastrophe: A Selected and Annotated Bibliography* (1962); vols. 5–8: M. Piekarz et al. (eds.), *The Jewish Holocaust and Heroism Through the Eyes of the Hebrew Press* (1966); vols. 9, 10: J. Gar, *Bibliography of Articles on the Catastrophe and Heroism in Yiddish Periodicals* (1966); Wiener Library Catalogue Series: (1) *Persecution and Resistance under the Nazis* (1960[2]); (2) *From Weimar to Hitler Germany 1918–1933* (1964[2]), 200–400; (4) *After Hitler, Germany 1945–1963* (1963); Bibliothèque du Centre de Documentation Juive Contemporaine, *Catalogue,* no. 1 (1964), 43–229; no. 2 (1968), 20–174, 191–201, 208–12; B. Mark, *Męczeństwo i walka Żydów w latach okupacji* (1963), an annotated bibliography of literature in Polish.

(4) SPECIALIZED PERIODICALS: *Wiener Library Bulletin (WLB)* (1946–   ); *Yearbook of the Leo Baeck Institute* (1956–   ); Yad Vashem, *Bulletin* (1957–1968; new series 1969–   ); *Yedi'ot Yad Vashem* (1954–1968; new series 1969–   ); Yad Vashem, *Yedies* (1957–61); Yad Vashem, *Studies* (1957–   ); *Koveẓ Meḥkarim be-Farshiyot ha-Sho'ah*

ve-ha-Gevurah (1957–   ); Beit Loḥamei ha-Getta'ot, *Yedi'ot* (1951–60), *Dappim le-Ḥeker ha-Sho'ah* (1951–52, 1969); *Fun Letstn Khurbn* (1946–48); *Bleter far Geshikhte* (1948–   ); *Biuletyn Zydowskiego Instytutu Historycznego (BZIH)* (1951–   ); *Le Monde Juif* (1946–   ); *Gli ebrei in Italia durante il Fascismo*, 1–3 (1960–63).

(5) COLLECTIONS OF DOCUMENTS: S. Krieger (comp.), *Nazi Germany's War Against the Jews* (1947); L. Poliakov and J. Wulf, *Das Dritte Reich und die Juden: Dokumente und Aufsaetze* (1955²); idem, *Das Dritte Reich und seine Diener: Dokumente* (1956); idem, *Das Dritte Reich und seine Denker* (1959).

BIBLIOGRAPHY

Holocaust: GENERAL: chapt. 14. BEHAVIOR: K. Shabbetai, *As Sheep to the Slaughter* (1962); R. Hilberg, *Destruction of the European Jews* (1961, paperback 1967); N. Eck, in: *Yad Vashem Studies*, 6 (1967), 385–430; J. Robinson, *ibid.*, 7 (1968), 198–203; idem, *Psychoanalysis in a Vacuum, Bruno Bettelheim and the Holocaust* (1970); idem, *And the Crooked Shall be Made Straight* (1965), 142–226; idem, *Nittuk Reẓifui be-Va'adei ha-Kehillot ba-Tekufah ha-Naẓit* (1966); B. Bettelheim, *The Informed Heart, Autonomy in a Mass Age* (1960); idem, in: *Midstream*, 8 (Spring 1962), 16–25; A. L. Kubovy, in: *Yad Vashem Bulletin*, 13 (1963), 3–11; I. Poliakov, in: *Commentary*, 9 (Aug. 1950), 111–6; G. Hausner, *Justice in Jerusalem* (1966), 176–225; A. Berman, in: *Biuletyn Żydowskiego Instytutu Historycznego*, 29 (1959), 40–57 (Hebrew translation in N. Blumenthal and J. Kermisz, *Ha-Meri ve-ha-Mered be-Getto Varshah* (1965), 52–65); E. A. Cohen, *Human Behavior in the Concentration Camps* (1953); B. Kautsky, *Teufel und Verdammte* (1946), 153–9, 193–5; V. E. Frankl, *Man's Search for Meaning* (1967), 1–96; R. Hoess, *Commandant of Auschwitz* (1959), autobiography; K. Kromiadi, in: *Novy Zhurnal*, 32 (1953), 192–202; J. F. Steiner, *Treblinka* (Eng., 1967); P. Friedman, in: *Meẓudah*, 7 (1954), 602–18; idem, in: *Bitzaron*, 28 (1953), 29–40; 29 (1954), 151–8, 232–9; idem, in: *Yad Vashem Studies*, 2 (1958), 95–113; idem, in: J. L. Blau et al. (eds.), *Essays on Jewish Life and Thought* ... (1959), 190–230; H. Arendt, *Eichmann in Jerusalem* (1963), 102–7; D. Daube, *Collaboration with Tyranny in Rabbinical Law* (1965).

Concentration Camps: International Tracing Service, *Catalogue of Camps and Prisons in Germany and German-Occupied Territories*, 2 vols. (1949–51); idem, *Vorlaeufiges Verzeichnis der Konzentrationslager* ... (1969); International Military Tribunal, *Trial of the Major War Criminals*, 42 vols. (1947–49); idem, *Trial of*

German Major War Criminals, 23 vols. (1946–51); Jewish Black Book Committee, *Black Book* (1946); E. Kogon, *Theory and Practice of Hell* (1950); G. Reitlinger, *Final Solution* (1968²); R. Hoess, *Commandant of Auschwitz* (1959); H. Krausnick et al., *Anatomy of the SS State* (1968), 397–504; H. G. Adler, in: *World Congress of Jewish Studies. Papers*, 1 (1967), 27–31; A. Ungerer, *Verzeichnis von Ghettos, Zwangsarbeitslagern und Konzentrationslagern . . .* (1953); E. Kossoy and E. Hammitsch, *Handbuch zum Entschaedigungsverfahren* (1958); R. Hilberg, *The Destruction of the European Jews* (1961).

Gassing: R. Hilberg, *Destruction of the European Jews* (1967), index; G. Reitlinger, *Final Solution* (1968²), 130–64 and index; M. Weinreich, *Hitler's Professors* (1946), passim; A. Mitscherlich and F. Mielke, *Doctors of Infamy* (1949); K. Binding and A. Hoche, *Die Freigabe der Vernichtung unwerten Lebens, ihr Mass und ihre Form* (1920, 1922²); *Trials of War Criminals . . .*, 1 (1949); *Anklageschrift des Generalstaatsanwalt Frankfurt a. M. gegen den frueheren Arzt Horst Schuman von 12. 12. 1969*, Yad Vashem, no. 0404/20–83; K. Doerner, in: *Vierteljahrhefte fuer Zeitgeschichte*, 15 (1967), no. 2, 121–52.

Adolf Hitler: Hitler's speeches are recorded in *Speeches of Adolf Hitler, 1922–39* (ed. N. H. Baynes, 1942), and in *Hitler: Reden und Proklamationen, 1939–45*, by M. Domarus (2 vols., 1962–63); F. Heer, *Der Glaube des Adolf Hitler* (1968), includes bibliography; G. Reitlinger, *Final Solution* (1968²), index; W. Maser, *Die Fruehgeschichte der NSDAP: Hitlers Weg bis 1924* (1965); H. Trevor-Roper (ed.), *Hitler's War Directives* (1964); A. Bullock, *Hitler: A Study in Tyranny* (1962²); R. Hilberg, *Destruction of the European Jews* (1961), index; F. Jetzinger, *Hitler's Youth* (1958); J. Tenenbaum, *Race and Reich* (1956), index; A. Kubizek, *Young Hitler I Knew* (1954); H. R. Trevor-Roper (ed.), *Hitler Table Talk 1941–44* (1953); H. Rauschning, *Hitler Speaks* (1939).

Partisans: Y. Suhl (ed.), *They Fought Back* (1968); J. Robinson, *And the Crooked Shall be Made Straight* (1965), 213–26 and index; *European Resistance Movements 1939–1945*, 1 (1960), 2 (1964), passim; *Sefer Milhamot ha-Getta'ot* (1954² = *The Fighting Ghettos*, partial trans. by M. Barkai, 1962); M. Kahanovich, in: *Yad Vashem Studies*, 1 (1957), 153–67; A. Z. Bar-On, *ibid.* (1960),

167–89; J. Ariel, *ibid.*, 6 (1967), 221–50; H. Michel, *ibid.*, 7 (1968), 1–16; *Sefer ha-Partizanim ha-Yehudim*, 2 vols. (1958); A. Lidowski, *Ba-Ye'arot* (1946); R. Korchak, *Lehavot ba-Efer* (1956); A. Z. Bar-On and D. Levin, *Toledoteha shel Maḥteret* (1962); K. Nir, *Shevilim be-Ma'gal ha-Esh* (1967); B. West, *Hem Hayu Rabbim* (1968); Y. Yelinek, in: *Yalkut Moreshet*, 1 no. 1 (1963), 47–67 (Eng. summ.); H. Smolar, *Yidn in Gele Lates* (1952²); D. Knout, *Contribution à l'histoire de la résistance juive en France, 1940–1944* (1967).

Rescue: A. D. Morse, *While Six Million Died* (1968); A. Weissberg, *Conspiracy of Silence* (1952); S. Kot, *Conversations with the Kremlin and Dispatches from Russia* (1963); U. S. Department of State, Publication 3023, *Nazi-Soviet Relations 1939–1942* (1948); Polish Embassy in USSR, *Report on the Relief Accorded to Polish Citizens* ... (1943); N. Bentwich, *Wanderer Between Two Worlds* (1941); P. Meyer et al., *Jews in the Soviet Satellites* (1953); R. Hilberg, *Destruction of the European Jews* (1961), 715–33; L. Yahil, *Rescue of Danish Jewry* (1969); M. B. Weissmandel, *Min ha-Meẓar* (1957); Y. Bauer, *From Diplomacy to Resistance* (1970), passim; M. Kaganovich, *Di Milkhome fun Yidishe Partizaner in Mizrekh Eyrope* (1956); H. Smolar, *Fun Minsker Geto* (1946); S. Kacherginsky, *Tsvishn Hamer un Serp* (1949); E. Landau (ed.), *Der Kastner Bericht* ... (1961); S. M. Schwarz, *Yevrei v Sovetskom Soyuze, 1939–1965* (1966).

Christian Churches: CATHOLIC CHURCH: S. Friedlaender, *Pius XII and the Third Reich* (1966); G. Lewy, *Catholic Church and Nazi Germany* (1964), ch. 10; P. Blet et al. (eds.), *Lettres de Pie XII aux évêques allemands* (1966); E. Bentley (ed.), *Storm Over the Deputy* (1964), incl. bibl.; J. Nobécourt, *"Le Vicaire" et l'histoire* (1964); Rothkirchen, in: *Yad Vashem Studies*, 6 (1967), 27–53; P. Friedman, *Their Brothers' Keepers* (1957); M. Faulhaber, *Judaism, Christianity and Germany* (1934); Carpi, in: *Yad Vashem Studies*, 4 (1960), 43–56; Lewy, in: *Commentary*, 37 no. 2 (1964), 23–35; J. S. Conway, *The Nazi Persecution of the Churches, 1933–1945* (1968). PROTESTANT AND GREEK ORTHODOX CHURCHES: J. M. Snoek, *The Grey Book* ... (1969), incl. bibl.; W. A. Visser 't Hooft, *Struggle for the Dutch Church* ... (1944); *Les Eglises Protestantes pendant la guerre et l'occupation* (1946); *Die Evangelische Kirche in Deutschland und die Judenfrage* (1945); M. Leviev, *Nashata Blagodarnost* (Bul., n. d.).

War Crimes Trials: *History of the United Nations War Crimes Commission* (1948); World Jewish Congress, *Unity in Dispersion* (1948); J. Robinson, *And the Crooked Shall be Made Straight* (1965); idem and P. Friedman, *Guide to Jewish History under the Nazi Impact* (1960), 176–221; idem, in: *Kovez Mehkarim ba-Mishpat ha-Beinle'ummi ha-Pumbi le-Zekher Sir Hersch Lauterpacht* (1961), 84–91; N. Robinson, *Report on the Activities of the Institute of Jewish Affairs, World Jewish Congress, in the Field of the Prosecution of War Criminals in Germany* (1961); idem, in: *Gesher,* 7 no. 2 (1961), 38–50; idem, in: *Le Monde Juif,* 26, no. 60/61 (1971), 16–23; E. Brand, in: *Yad Vashem Bulletin,* 14 (1964), 58–62, 19 (1966), 36–44, 20 (1967), 14–29, 21 (1967), 18–21; Lévai, in: R. L. Braham (ed.), *Hungarian Jewish Studies,* (1969), 253–96, German Federal Republic, Bundesministerium fuer Justiz, *Die Verfolgung nationalsozialistischer Straftaten im Gebiet der Bundesrepublik Deutschland seit 1945* (1964); R. Vogel (ed.), *Ein Weg aus der Vergangenheit: Eine Dokumentation zur Verjaehrungsfrage und zu den nationalsozialistischen Prozessen* (1969), *Probleme der Verfolgung und Ahndung von nationalsozialistischen Gewaltverbrechen* (1967); R. Henkys, *Die nationalsozialistischen Gewaltverbrechen* (1964); Deutscher Bundestag, *175. Sitzung, Bonn, 25. 3. 1965;* J. Gorzkowska and E. Zakowska, *Zbrodniarze hitlerowscy przed sądami NRF* (1964); N. S. Alekseyev, *Otvetstvennost natsistskikh prestupnikov* (1968).

Adolf Eichmann: The Eichmann trial English transcripts were made available by Microcard Edition, Washington, D.C. in 65 microcards. R. L. Braham, *The Eichmann Case: A Source Book* (1969); Israel Government Press Office, *Adolf Eichmann's Statement at the Police* (1961), in German; J. Lévai, *Eichmann in Hungary: Documents* (1961); G. Hausner (state prosecutor), *Opening Statement: "6,000,000 Accusers"* (1961); Ha-Yo'ez ha-Mishpati la-Memshalah neged Adolf Eichmann, *Eduyyot,* 2 vols. (1963); idem, *Ne'um ha-Sikkum* (1962); *International Law Reports,* 36 (1968), 18–344; M. Pearlman, *Capture and Trial of Adolf Eichmann* (1963); G. Hausner, *Justice in Jerusalem* (1968²); H. Arendt, *Eichmann in Jerusalem* (1965²); J. Robinson, *And the Crooked Shall Be Made Straight* (1962); Lord Russell of Liverpool, *Trial of Adolf Eichmann . . .* (1962); R. M. W. Kempner, *Ha-Mikzo'a Hashmadah: Darko shel Eichmann* (1963); Simon and Donat, in: *Judaism,* 12 (1963), 387–435; *American Jewish Year Book,* 63 (1962), 3–131; 64 (1963), 247–59; J. E. C. Fawcett, in: **201**

British Year-Book of International Law, 38 (1962), 18ı
Schwarzenberger, in: *Current Legal Problems,* 15 (1962), 248–6ɔ
Treves, in: *Minnesota Law Review,* 47 (1962), 557–92; Green, in:
Tulane Law Review, 37 (1962/63), 641–84.

Soviet Russia: E. Litvinoff (ed.), *Jews in Eastern Europe;* S.
M. Schwarz, *Yevrei v Sovetskom Soyuze, 1939–1965* (1966).

Jewish Consciousness after the Holocaust: I. Maybaum, *The Face
of God after Auschwitz* (1965); *The Seventh Day, Soldiers Talk
about the Six-Day War* (1970); H. Arendt, *Eichmann in Jerusalem*
(1963); "Jewish Values in the Post-Holocaust Future," a sym-
posium, in: *Judaism,* 16, no. 3 (Summer, 1967); G. Steiner,
in: *Encounter,* v. 28, no. 2 (February 1967); E. L. Fackenheim, in:
Commentary, v. 46, no. 2 (August, 1968); *"The Impact of the
Holocaust," in: Commentary,* v. 46, no. 2 (August, 1968); The
Institute of Contemporary Jewry, *The Impact of the Holocaust
on Contemporary Jewish Life* (1972) (Hebrew); U. Tal,
Self-Understanding and the Land and State of Israel," in: *Union
Seminary Quarterly Review,* v. 26, no. 4 (Summer, 1971); G.
Scholem, "Reflections on the Possibility of Jewish Mysticism
in our Time," in: *Ariel,* no. 26 (1970); Y. Bauer and E. Schweid,
in: *Sh'demoth,* no. 38, 39, 40 (Hebrew); U. Ramon, "Holocaust
Consciousness during the Six Day War," in: *Dappim, Studies
of the Holocaust and the Jewish Resistance,* Second Series, v. 1
(1969) (Hebrew with English summary).

GLOSSARY

Aktion (Ger.), operation involving the mass assembly, deportation, and murder of Jews by the Nazis during the Holocaust.

American Jewish Joint Distribution Committee (popularly known as the JDC or the "Joint"), American Jewry's overseas relief and rehabilitation agency founded in 1914.

Anschluss (Ger. "annexation"), annexation of Austria to Germany on March 13, 1938.

Beriḥah ("flight"), name of organized underground operation moving Jews out of Eastern Europe, USSR, Balkan, and Baltic countries, into central and Southern Europe between 1944 and 1948, as a step toward their—mostly "illegal"—immigration to Palestine; also name of spontaneous mass movement of Jewish survivors from Europe toward Ereẓ Israel.

Bermuda Conference, Anglo-American Conference on refugees held in Bermuda April 19–30, 1943.

Bernheim Petition, petition against Nazi anti-Jewish legislation in German Upper Silesia, signed by Franz Bernheim, a warehouse employee in Upper Silesia, and submitted to the League of Nations on May 17, 1933.

Betar, Zionist youth movement of the Zionist Revisionist party (now of Ḥerut movement).

Boycott (anti-Jewish), organized activity in Nazi Germany directed against the Jews to exclude them from social, economic, and political life.

Bund, Jewish socialist party founded in Russia (1897), devoted to Yiddish, autonomism, secular Jewish nationalism, and sharply opposed to Zionism.

Centos, Polish organization for the care of orphans.

Deror, Zionist-socialist pioneering youth movement.

Der Stuermer ("the assailant"), anti-Semitic German weekly, founded and edited by Julius Streicher, appeared in Nuremberg between 1923 and 1945.

Displaced Persons (DPs), term used to describe people who had been driven out of their homes as a result of Nazi decrees and WW II.

Einsatzgruppen, mobile units of the Nazi S.S. and S.D.; in Russia and Serbia, mobile killing units.

Europa Plan, scheme for the ransom of about 1,000,000 Jews remaining in Europe to save them from extermination, initiated by the "Working Group" of Bratislava in autumn of 1942.

Evian Conference, conference on refugee problems held at Evian-les-Bains in France in July 1938 by representatives of 31 countries.

Final Solution (Ger. *Endloesung*), in Nazi terminology, the Nazi-planned mass murder and total annihilation of the Jews.

General Government, territory in Poland administered by a German civilian governor–general with headquarters in Cracow after the German occupation in World War II.

Genocide, the partial or entire destruction of religious, racial, or national groups.

Gordonia, pioneering Zionist youth movement.

Haavara, a company for the transfer of Jewish property from Nazi Germany to Palestine, established in Tel Aviv in August 1933.

Ha-Shomer Ha-Za'ir, Zionist-socialist pioneering youth movement.

He-Halutz, Zionist pioneer youth association founded in many countries.

HICEM, emigration association set up in 1927 by various Jewish organizations (HIAS, ICA, Emigdirect).

Institute of Jewish Affairs, research institute set up in 1940 by the World Jewish Congress.

Jewish Agency, international, nongovernment body, centered in Jerusalem; the executive and representative of World Zionist Organization.

Jewish Brigade, infantry brigade group formed as part of the British army in September 1944.

Judenrat, council of Jewish representatives set up in communities and ghettos under the Nazis to execute their instructions.

Judenrein, a locality from which all Jews had been eliminated.

Juedischer Kulturbund, German Jewish organization founded in Berlin in May 1933, to spread interest in Jewish art and culture in Nazi Germany. It was discontinued in October 1938.

Kapo, prisoner in charge of a group of inmates in Nazi concentration camps.

Kristallnacht (Ger. "crystal night," meaning "night of broken glass"), organized destruction of synagogues, Jewish houses, and shops, accompanied by arrests of individual Jews, which took place in Germany and Austria under the Nazis on the night of Nov. 9–10, 1938.

Madagascar Plan, Nazi plan to evacuate 4,000,000 Jews to Madagascar over a period of four years. It was taken up in summer 1940, but shelved in Feb. 10, 1942, after the Nazis decided to carry out the "Final Solution."

Mein Kampf, title of work written by Adolf Hitler (1925–27), setting forth his political program.

Munich Agreement (or Munich Pact), agreement made at Munich between Hitler, Chamberlain, Mussolini, and Daladier on Sept. 30, 1938, providing for the cession of the Sudetenland by Czechoslovakia to Germany.

Muselmann, Nazi camp slang word for prisoner on the brink of death.

Nuremberg Laws, Nazi laws excluding Jews from German citizenship.

Po'alei Zion, Zionist-socialist movement.

Protocols of the "Elders of Zion", anti-Semitic forgery aimed at showing the existence of international Jewish aspiration bent on world power. It was concocted in the last decade of the 19th c. by an unknown author working for the Russian secret police.

Reichsvereinigung, compulsory organization of all Jews in Nazi Germany (excepting Austria and the Protectorate of Bohemia-Moravia), established on July 4, 1939, in accordance with the Reich's citizenship law.

Reichsvertretung der Juden in Deutschland, voluntary organization founded in 1933 in Berlin. Its main task was to organize emigration of Jews from Germany. It was replaced in 1939 by the Reichsvereinigung.

Reichszentrale fuer Juedische Auswanderung, Nazi central agency for Jewish emigration matters, set up in German Ministry of Interior on Jan. 14, 1939.

Righteous of the Nations, term applied to those non-Jews who saved Jews from their Nazi persecutors at the risk of their own lives.

R.S.H.A. (initials of Ger. Reichssicherheitshauptamt), the central security department of German Reich, formed in 1939, and combining the security police and the S.D.

S.A. (abb. **Sturm Abteilungen**), the storm troops of the early Nazi party, organized in 1922.

S.D. (abb. **Sicherheitsdienst**), security service of the S.S. formed in 1932 as the sole intelligence organization of the Nazi party.

S.S. (abb. **Schutzstaffel**), Nazi formation established in 1925 which later became the "elite" organization of the Nazi party and carried out central tasks in the "Final Solution."

Struma, name of a boat carrying 769 Jewish refugees, which left Rumania late in 1941, was refused entry to Palestine or Turkey, and sank in the Black Sea in Feb. 1942, with the loss of all on board except one.

Third Reich, term applied to National Socialist (Nazi) Germany.

TOZ, Jewish welfare organization in Poland.

Va'ad Ha-Haẓalah, Jewish rescue committees that functioned in different countries in Europe during the Holocaust.

Wannsee Conference, the Nazi conference held in Wannsee, Berlin, on Jan. 20, 1942, which decided to carry out the "Final Solution."

War Refugee Board, a U.S. government special agency for rescue of and aid to WW II victims, established on Jan. 22, 1944, by U.S. President Roosevelt.

Wehrmacht, German armed forces.

White Paper 1939, a British government statement of Palestine policy, which restricted Jewish immigration to Palestine, and prohibited purchase of land by Jews there.

World Jewish Congress, a voluntary association of representative Jewish bodies, communities, and organizations throughout the world, established in 1936.

Yad Vashem, Israel official authority for commemorating the Holocaust in the Nazi era and Jewish resistance and heroism at that time.

Yellow Badge, distinctive sign which, by Nazi order, was compulsorily worn by Jews.

Zaddik (pl. **zaddikim**), a ḥasidic rabbi or leader.

INDEX